THE AFFABLE ENEMY

The Affable Enemy

by
Wallace E. Fisher

ABINGDON PRESS
Nashville and New York

THE AFFABLE ENEMY

Copyright © 1970 by Abingdon Press

Standard Book Number: 687-00949-9

Library of Congress Catalog Card Number: 71-97567

SET UP, PRINTED, AND BOUND BY THE
PARTHENON PRESS, AT NASHVILLE,
TENNESSEE, UNITED STATES OF AMERICA

To the hundreds of thousands of educated, successful, community-minded men in the church *who—if they put their splendid talents and worldly experience at Christ's disposal—have it in their power to make thousands of parishes effective instruments of reconciliation* now.

PREFACE

This is a collection of correspondence between a business executive and his former teacher, a university professor. It spans a decade and a half—1969 to 1984. It focuses on the church, Christianity, and the world. Reading other people's mail can be fascinating—and quite respectable when it is shared for a public reading. This particular correspondence will be more enlightening if the reader scans the table of contents and reads the introduction before he digs into the letters.

Some patient laymen from several religious traditions (Baptist, Episcopal, Lutheran, Quaker, Roman Catholic, Unitarian, United Church of Christ, United Methodist, and United Presbyterian), and some who stand outside any religious tradition, aided in editing this correspondence: Terry Abrams, William and Mary Atlee, Wilfred and Jean Bennett, William and Jean Brenner, Henry and Jane Brown, Robert and Sally Desch, Melvin and Sonya Evans, Nancy Fellenbaum, Carl E. Fisher, Robert and Nancy Gates, Paul and Sylvia Hollinger, Ruth Grigg Horting, Alex and Elizabeth Leidy, William and Marilyn Luff, John M. Martin, Jr., Albert and Carole Mattison, Bruce McClellan, Robert Moore, Paul and Jane Mueller, Elvin and

Ann Musselman, Harold and Olive Quickel, Kenneth and Helen Shelley, George E. Spencer, Kirk and Ann White, and Robert and Doris Witmer. Among them are business executives, professors, public school teachers, medical doctors, lawyers, radio station managers, engineers, chemists, nurses, community chest executives, a bookseller, a headmaster, a theater manager, a former member of a governor's cabinet, a former actress, and homemakers.

Jack R. Hoffman and Vincent R. Eshelman, ministerial colleagues at the Lutheran Church of the Holy Trinity; R. Ray Evelan and Larry L. Lehman, former colleagues at Trinity; Jack Kirk, Harald S. Sigmar, Byron Stroh, and Elton Trueblood, ministerial friends in Greensboro, North Carolina; Tacoma, Washington; Indianapolis and Richmond, Indiana, offered valuable insights. Mrs. Arline Fellenbaum, my secretary, prepared the manuscript. My wife, Margaret Elizabeth, and our son, Mark, now accustomed to a writer in the household, were especially enthusiastic about this venture and, as always, provided understanding, generous support and constructive criticism.

WALLACE E. FISHER

CONTENTS

INTRODUCTION

In three previous books I have reported on a twelve-year renewal program in an urban church (*From Tradition to Mission*), provided a clinical appraisal of preaching as a function of ministry in ongoing parish renewal (*Preaching and Parish Renewal*), and offered a concise study guide on congregational renewal for laymen (*Preface to Parish Renewal*). Those books, generously received in Protestant circles, concentrate on content *and* form, spirit *and* structure. This book focuses on content and spirit. The significance of worship forms and ecclesiastical structures is implicit in the presentation.

Casual commitment to Christ, compartmentalized religion, and anti-intellectualism—triple threats to a relevant Christian witness—are addressed in popular language. The argument centers on the implications of the Christian Faith for life: marriage, family, vocation, churchmanship, citizenship. It also focuses on the relationship between witness and worship, the authority of Scripture and tradition, the nature and language of faith. In this generation, the church must tackle human concerns (poverty, discrimination, war and peace), but unless it also concentrates on God's concern for the whole man it is not the church. Unless it proclaims and demonstrates the presence of the redeeming God in *our* history, it is not the church. The old controversy over *faith* and good works, *doctrine* and deeds, has suddenly come alive in the closing decades of the twentieth century. It is as crucial to a relevant church now as it was in the sixteenth century or the fourth century.

It was needful to call the twentieth-century church to sacrificial involvement in the world. It was needful to remind the contemporary church that it exists to serve God and man here and now. But, if the church is to be transformed from little bands of commandos into a disciplined army, if it is to move beyond morbid self-examination and sporadic social involvement, it is imperative that a corps of laity in each congregation wrestle intellectually with ethical and doctrinal questions in the light of the gospel. There is a place for serious "God-talk," the Anglo-Saxon equivalent for "theology." The church's mission is to help the dispossessed, the possessors, and the "possessed" from the resources of the gospel. Denis de Rougemont argues cogently that today's earnest Christian finds himself in a situation that is utterly insane: a world where the faith "is denied, more or less serenely ignored, or, even worse, where Christianity is accepted and ridiculed under the form of its traditional deviations, its caricatures; in short, in a world where it does not exist." [1] This situation will not change substantially unless the church ventures boldly into the world for Christ and, developing a new taste for ideas and concepts, presents intelligibly its manifesto for doing so. The American Revolution would have been stillborn without the sacrificial deeds of men in the field and the courageous involvement of leaders in every colony. But that revolution would have sputtered ineffectually or fragmented colonial society if the ideological writings of Locke and Montesquieu, Jefferson and Adams, Hamilton and Madison had not permeated the daily thoughts and conversations of thousands of citizens in the thirteen colonies.

To get the case for good works and *faith*—deeds and *doctrine*—before critical-minded laymen I have employed an old literary device: the exchange of letters. The correspondence is between a university professor and a successful executive, his former student. The professorial correspondent, James Johnson, owes his person to three creative teachers I have been privileged to know. Two guided me in the graduate schools of the Universities of Pennsylvania and Pittsburgh. The third was an esteemed colleague on the faculty at Gettysburg College during a season when I had deliberately turned my back on the parish ministry. Tough-minded, large-spirited, respectful of a man's freedom, a devotee of religionless Christianity before *that* was fashionable, he was an admirable devil's advocate.

The other correspondent, Theodore Connors, owes his brash style, alert mind, and resilient spirit to countless influential laymen I know and have known through participation in a hundred or so renewal conferences across the nation and through seventeen years in a socially heterogeneous urban church. These co-authors remain nameless, but I am indebted to them for Ted. He is the solid American: usually a veteran, college-educated or self-educated, at home with ideas and images, vocationally competent, pious and secular, comfortable in his family commitments, and politically stable—too intellectual to be an extreme rightist, too pragmatic to be an ultra-liberal. This solid American, when he unites with the church as hundreds of thousands do, usually settles for casual commitment to Christ, displays a remarkable talent for unconscious subversion, and often slides into spectatorism. This Affable Enemy must be identified, unmasked, persuaded to serious commitment, and nurtured in that commitment. Otherwise, the community of believers' sporadic involvements in contemporary society will wane as they did when World War I torpedoed the social gospel.

The opening letters in this collection exaggerate what many laymen do unconsciously—subvert the Christian community. These laymen—uninformed on the nature of biblical faith, disposed to view ecclesiastical forms as ends rather than means, and theologically naïve—are Affable Enemies. Professor Johnson, tongue in cheek, defines the face of the enemy in a series of letters calling for deliberate subversion. This overdrawn description of parish life gives way quickly to a serious exchange of views, ideas, and convictions between Johnson and Connors as each, in different crisis situations, faces his personal needs and discovers new human possibilities through an existential relationship with Christ. How this faith comes, the nurturing of it, and the fruits of it inform this part of the correspondence. After all, becoming committed is not the same as staying committed. Indifference, like unconscious subversion, is insidious. Both evils, masked by affability, can make the church an anachronism in a technological, revolutionary society.

The letters are written primarily for laymen who have a taste for ideas and an interest in language—a substantial segment in most congregations. These restless people must be persuaded to dig into the Scriptures and the church's teachings. They must be equipped to use both creatively. Their outspoken criticisms of the church's current teachings (content, language, logic) must be heard and considered, challenged or affirmed. Laymen who think for themselves will not be lackeys in the church. They will not affirm static moral dogmas. They will not respond intellectually to shallow homilies on religion. They will not get existentially involved with Christ through evangelistic programs designed to "con" newcomers into joining the local parish. The popular response to studies like *Honest to God, The Secular City, Situation Ethics,* and writings from and on Vatican II, demonstrate plainly that laymen are willing and able to discuss Christian doctrine and ethics.

No less significant is the fact that many people outside the church—fascinated and confused by the tempo of social change; at odds with a traditional view of war as part of diplomacy between sovereign states; increasingly sensitive to the dehumanizing forces inherent in poverty, institutional bureaucracy, and status society; and searching for authentic values in an age of relativism—are addressing issues that are eschatological as well as mundane. Paul Goodman suggested recently that alienated persons in our society are asking theological questions more earnestly than many church members are. It is the local congregation's responsibility and privilege to get where *this* action is in community after community. The world is eager for dialogue when it is set in the context of concerned action and framed in a language that communicates reality. But *that* dialogue will be stillborn unless Christian laymen learn to carry their end of it.

I

THE FACE OF THE ENEMY

Socrates taught that the unexamined life is not worth living.

Paul called men to self-examination in the presence of that authentic Man, Jesus of Nazareth.

Ian McLaren preached that the Kingdom of God is not for the well-meaning but for the desperate.

New Canaan, Connecticut
6 February, 1969

Dear Ted,

What a pleasant surprise—hearing from you after all these years. Of course, there have been the annual Christmas cards, birth announcements, a hurried visit at Homecoming several years after your graduation, and the Alumni Journal's reports on your meteoric rise in a major corporation. Your alma mater is proud of you. Its administrative officers have their eye on you for a place on the Board of Governors— and, I suspect, a whopping contribution! You are remembered vividly at this University: decorated boy pilot home from World War II, distinguished student, skillful campus politician. I also remember you in our class discussions as a hard-nosed biblical literalist who insisted that Christian values can inform political decisions, guide military alliances, and create peaceful co-existence. In all this, you reminded me of an "intellectual" Eddie Rickenbacker. Of course, you did provide a preview of what shortly materialized in Foster Dulles' approach in international affairs during the fumbling 1950's!

Now, having discovered the anti-intellectual character of your Christian beliefs, you have decided to renounce them. Having recognized that the church's institutional self-protectiveness devours its members' time and talent, you are preparing to sever your allegiance to it. Having discerned the church's antiquated teachings, programmed activism, and narcissistic preoccupation with institutional security, you want its members freed to join secularists in building a rational society. Splendid! You have come of age. Your angry but

19

solidly reasoned critiques of the church reflect your new maturity.

But your judgment that "the church is excess baggage for those who want to build the Good Society" is too sanguine. The church is absolute *dead weight*. Its white, middle-class members use organized religion as a sanction for their privileges, a bulwark for their possessions, a screen for their uninvolvement with hard-pressed persons, and a cover for their thinly veiled refusal to face unpalatable historical realities. Culturally and historically the American parish is the last refuge of unbridled individualism in our society. There a man who feels frustrated and cramped by the external disciplines imposed by family, job, or citizenship feels free to exercise unrestrained authority. What church members piously call "the priesthood of believers" is in reality an association of people determined to say and do what each feels is in the interests of himself and his own group. Protestants have distorted that Reformation doctrine into an "everyman-his-own-boss" doctrine. Neither clergy nor laity accept their Christ as a sovereign over Scripture or church, let alone society. Their vaunted "Word of God" is used as a crutch for insecure persons or as a platform on which empty people rise to positions of power and prestige in the little world of their parish, diocese, or denominational hierarchy. Many undisciplined church members use "the Word" as a blunt instrument to bludgeon those who differ from them doctrinally and morally and, often of late, economically and politically. The church destroys initiative, smothers free inquiry, resists change. Consequently, it impedes social, economic, and political progress.

Remembering my critiques of Christianity and the church during your poli-sci courses here at the University, you now seek my support in attacking the church. Agreed—the alliance is formed.

Don't leave the church; subvert it from within. Marshal the unconscious subversives in its ranks. The church can be renewed or disabled most effectively at the grass roots. Launch a devious attack on its teachings, practices, clerical and lay leadership, and general membership. I'll help you mount this four-pronged assault.

Cordially,

James Johnson

II

Chicago, Illinois
16 February, 1969

Dear Prof,

You haven't changed over the years. Your response, like your class lectures, was clearheaded and decisive. But you are too quick for me. Take it in easy stages!

My disenchantment with the church as a social institution and with Christianity as a way of living has been gradual. So has my wife's. Joan and I were reared in hard-nosed Calvinist churches. Neither of us examined his faith or looked honestly at congregational life until a few years ago. You recall how stubbornly I resisted your critiques of Christianity and the church when I was a student. But Joan and I *did* examine Christianity and the church critically when our oldest child, after eight weeks' instruction in the Faith, became a thirteen-year-old communicant in this congregation. Her questions forced us to face what we had known but refused to admit for some years: this congregation's constructive involvement in society is negligible. Christianity is not an authentic creed for heroes in this era.

Joan and I are appalled at our belated recognition that Christian teaching is irrelevant and that the church is a parasitic social institution. We want to liberate others from that irrelevance and get them free of the ecclesiastical organization. First, however, we need to get our bearings. You can guide us, if you will.

Why did you leave the church in your youth? Why should I subvert an archaic institution? How do you justify subversion? It's un-American. Why not launch an open intellectual attack like Bertrand Russell's or Sigmund Freud's? It is necessary only to point out the obvious to most people these days.

Sincerely,

Ted

III

New Canaan, Connecticut
20 February, 1969

Dear Ted,

All right, we'll take it in three stages. What happened to my religion? Why did I choose humanism? How can the church's hold on middle-class America be broken?

Nothing in my youthful church experience had equipped me for my debilitating experiences in World War II—especially that shattering inspection of Dachau and the cloak-and-dagger months with our military government in sectored Berlin, 1945-46. The cumulative weight of those experiences crushed any notion I had that God is anyone's father! I decided that the only god who exists is the Clockmaker God of the Enlightenment—creator and regulator, uninvolved in human affairs, untouched by human tragedy. I decided that man is history's only hero and only villain. He not only acts out the script; he also writes and directs it. The evidence in war-ravaged Europe informed and shaped those conclusions, although I was leaning toward them when I enrolled in graduate school in 1940 to pursue a doctorate in English, hoping to teach and write. The war altered those plans.

During my years in the service I reflected seriously on man's capacity to create as well as his disposition to destroy. Increasingly aware of the significance of history, I became interested in political institutions and political theories. Convinced that what man can rationally conceive he can rationally create and maintain, I decided to get my doctorate in political science and government and to teach as a viable way to promote and safeguard social justice. Returning to earn my Ph.D. in political science rather than in English, I embraced humanism, scoffed at the University's beefed-up Department of Religion, declined to participate in any religious discussion on campus, and avoided preachers who spoke weekly at the University Chapel. During those years my intellectual critiques of the institutional church and its teaching were formed. When you enrolled in my classes I was an established professor who seized every opportunity to persuade students to bypass the church and ally themselves with humanists *and* political realists to create a humane society under law. I have since learned that strategy is inadequate. The church has a strange power to attract persons; it must be attacked from *within* if its crippling influence is to be curtailed.

DO NOT LEAVE THE CHURCH. Be a deliberate subversive. Use your place of leadership to discredit the Christian message, to undermine the parish leadership, and to disrupt the general membership.

When I quit the church in my mid-twenties I was convinced that my generation would defect en masse. I discovered that the hedgerows of France and the foxholes of Germany were peopled by rationalists, agnostics, atheists, and religious opportunists. I was sure that the church, discredited by the horrors brought on by Christian nations, would wither within a quarter-century. I erred spectacularly! Millions of Protestants and Roman Catholics in my generation flocked to the church after the war and served its narrow institutional aims. Suburban developers donated land, and church mission boards borrowed millions to build new churches for mobile America. A scattering of churchmen got involved with economically hard-pressed persons and tackled complex social issues, but most church members opted for "religion in general." The church's institutional life surged to new heights. Institutional ecumenism had a field day. Denominational mergers were frequent. Evangelism adopted the tactics of "hard sell." The Kirkentag attracted huge crowds in West Germany, and Billy Graham's crusade organizers accommodated tens of thousands in America's leading fun cities. Norman Vincent Peale, nationally syndicated, became the hero of a movie; and a religious best seller, *A Man Called Peter,* was turned into a soap opera for the big screen. Religion was an "in" thing.

Because of the religious boom in the 1940's and 1950's the American parish is presently strong numerically, organizationally, and economically. Its considerable influence will certainly continue. Peter Berger, a perceptive sociologist, predicts that within a few decades there will be only a handful of Christian believers huddled together in tiny sects as outposts resisting a worldwide secular culture. He expects that the occasional believer will be like "a Tibetan astrologer on a prolonged visit to an American university" who realizes finally that "the stars don't control reality after all." [1] I don't agree. Berger underestimates the stubborn resilience of the Christian illusion *and* the vast institutional strength it commands in America. Unless this entrenched social institution is subverted from within during the next decade, I predict that it will surge forward with vigor during the closing decades of this century. I expect that it will decline in numerical membership. There will be fewer congregations, but these will be larger, better staffed, and strengthened by regional coalitions across denominational lines. As Belgium was "cornered into heroism" during the early days of World War I, the church is now being forced into ecumenism at the grass roots. This "new" church will speak and act more effectively in society. Its tighter membership—disciplined, vocal, freshly conscious of its unique character—will be a menace in the revolutionary years ahead. Unless the church is fully domesticated *now,* a new generation will fall prey to its cannibalistic institutionalism and enervating supernaturalism.

Your place of leadership in a particular congregation is the ideal base for subversive attack. After all, most critics of the church during the 1960's were churchmen in good standing! John Robinson, popularizing Bultmann effectively and interpreting Bonhoeffer superficially, received a wide hearing, partly because he was an Anglican bishop. Cox, Winter, Marty, Hamilton, Van Buren, and Fletcher are professors in schools of theology. Bonhoeffer's radical critiques, overly studied and tiresomely quoted, are promoted by churchmen who talk more about that bold Christian than they emulate him. The critics *in* the church got the best hearing in the early 1960's. One suspects that overworked parish pastors, concerned theological professors, and hard-pressed bishops often prayed, "God, protect me from my friends; I can take care of my enemies!"

I'm not suggesting that these critics set out to undermine the church or the Faith. They challenged the institutional church to look compassionately on persons and present a relevant message in word and deed. In the process, some church critics created more heat than light in Christian circles. I appreciate Tom Driver's observation that "when the ethos of faith and purpose in Protestantism was strong, the seminary could play Socrates to the church's piety. But this is not possible when the church is on the defensive. The church today needs theological gadflies like it needs a locust plague." [2] But I don't concur in that judgment. The church critics rendered a significant service. They helped to deflate the absurd postwar religious boom. Their intellectual critiques of religion in general, faith in "faith," human piety, and otherworldliness reminded the church of its peculiar identity *and* the necessity of its witness *in* the world. That is precisely the kind of church that must be subverted. Remain in the church, Ted. Launch your assault deviously from within.

Admittedly, this Machiavellian *modus operandi* will be repugnant to you, but it works. Furthermore, it is woven into our national fabric. The hidden history of the CIA will not be fully written because it is Machiavellian. Our FBI agents, practiced Machiavellians, forfeit one raison d'etre if they are less the "masters of deceit" than the Communists. Our government's Machiavellian temper of mind surfaces occasionally: the U-2 incident, the Bay of Pigs, the Pueblo incident. Fictional thrillers, like *The Spy Who Came in From the Cold* and *Funeral in Berlin,* and factual exposés like *The Philby Conspiracy* are tracts of our times.

But such practices are realistic. The nineteenth century was relatively calm after the Congress of Vienna because political realists like Prince Metternich, Cavour, Disraeli, and Bismarck managed the affairs of sovereign states.[3] They were Machiavellian to the core. Cavour employed any means at hand to unify Italy. Disraeli duped Queen Victoria to get India for Britain. Bismarck tricked Napoleon III into the Franco-Prussian War. Lincoln—willing to free all, some, or none of the slaves in order to preserve the Union—was a hard-nosed political realist. On the other hand, Woodrow Wilson—too idealistic to play political poker with power politicians like Georges Clemenceau and Lloyd George, and too rigid to horse-trade with senators like Henry Cabot Lodge—dissipated America's then bright opportunity for creative world leadership.

The Communists are masters of the Machiavellian style. They did not attack the church head-on in postwar Europe. They did not imprison the anti-Nazi hero, Bishop Otto Dibelius, who served until his retirement in East Berlin; they ridiculed and harassed him. I remember a cartoon in an East Berlin newspaper which caricatured the Bishop as a bulky atomic bomb from America—an easy task for the cartoonist since Dibelius' physical appearance lent itself to that particular caricature. The Communists did not depose Bishop Lajos Ordass; they framed him. The Communists did not liquidate Joseph Hromadka in Prague; they out-maneuvered him. Hromadka's heartbroken letter to the Kremlin after the Soviet's oppressive measures against Czechoslovakia in 1968 is a tragic confession of misplaced confidence.[4]

Be Machiavellian. Distort the aims of committed Christians. Impugn their motives. Exploit their inevitable mistakes.

Do visit us when you come to New York on business. We are less than two hours by auto from Kennedy International.

Cordially,

Jim

P.S. Are you rebelling against the church because you're bored with your vocation or your family? Don't launch an attack unless you intend to see it through.

J.A.J.

IV

New Canaan
25 February, 1969

Dear Ted,

I didn't expect an answer by return mail, and I certainly didn't expect you to be miffed by the postscript. Has life in the corporation immunized you against candor on personal issues? Do you cherish the illusion that intellectual honesty exists apart from personal confrontation and personal decision? Even if I had framed that postscript more diplomatically, the basic issue to be faced would have remained unchanged. Either you attack or you don't. Yet you prefer to fondle contradictory views without giving yourself unreservedly to any particular view.

Four courses of action are open to you. One, resign your membership, leave quietly, and keep quiet. Presently, some laymen are doing that. Two, resign, present a bill of particulars against the church, and snipe at the institution from outside. Currently, that attack is rather popular. Three, don't make waves. Finish your term on the official board, attend services sporadically, complain occasionally, and stand clear. A host of laymen do that. Four, maintain your membership and attack subversively. That is the honorable course for you since you are convinced that Christianity and the church are inimical to the humane society.

Now, let me challenge your self-righteous judgment that the Machiavellian approach is un-American. You know better than that. I remember your anguished recollection of your part in the Dresden fire raid during a classroom discussion on the use of military power. Have you forgotten that? You knew then that the raid on Dresden served no military purpose. Participating in the establishment of military government in Germany, I helped to lay the foundation for the materialistic life that has developed in West Germany and, indirectly, for the austere life in East Germany. You and I, like our fellow-citizens, were involved in the nuclear destruction of Hiroshima and Nagasaki, even as the "innocent" German citizens were involved in the inhumanities committed at Dachau, Auschwitz, and Buchenwald. Americans are practiced Machiavellians. We canonize Paine, Henry, Adams, and Washington for ripping the Atlantic seaboard from their British benefactors. We approve Polk rather than Lincoln on the Mexican War (Manifest Destiny). Presently, we are struggling to live with the bitter heritage bequeathed by forebears who killed the American Indian or corralled him on reservations; forebears who enslaved the African, then freed but ghettoed him; and contemporaries who still resist the just demands of both minorities for sociopolitical structures in which they are free to

29

become human. Even Mr. Lincoln, committed to preserve the Union, adopted devious tactics to accomplish that end. Several years ago Dean Acheson, in a bold speech at Amherst College, stated plainly that our government is committed to employ any means (and does) if it judges that the end achieved will strengthen our national security.

The Machiavellian approach works. Use it in your parish.

Exasperatedly yours,

Jim

V

Chicago
27 February, 1969

Dear Prof,

I'm glad I wrote in anger and that you answered in the same vein. Your hard-nosed insistence on decision-making recalled yesteryear's exciting class hours. You argued cogently then that thought and action must be of a piece. You still do! But, decision-making on gut issues is tough for my generation. Certainly, it's difficult for me. My years in sales and management have conditioned me to be clever rather than critical-minded. I *am* skilled in Machiavellian practices—more so than I like to admit.

But my dilemma is situational as well as cultural. After all, I *am* responsible for marketing farm machinery. I'm paid to do that job, and if I fail at it, I'll be fired. Competition is the name of the game, man, and success provides me with a generous income. I like that. But there is more to it than that. Farm machinery is essential to our national economy. It is also essential to human existence here and throughout our overpopulated, technologically underdeveloped world. Your insinuation that businessmen have no social conscience is unfair. It is also hypocritical. The modern business community *and* the government insure *your* comfortable life at that prestigious "private" university!

Now let me answer your irritatingly personal questions. I'm not bored with my work. I like being a corporation vice-president. I've expanded sales 16 percent since taking over. The esprit de corps in my department doesn't match that of the old Eighth Air Force, but it's damned good! I like my vocation and the economic affluence it provides.

I've also examined my attitude toward marriage and family life. Extramarital escapades are run-of-the-mill in my social and business spheres. Reporting on these, John O'Hara is an accurate social historian as well as a rattling good storyteller! But I don't cheat, and neither does Joan; we have no desire to be unfaithful to each other. My marital behavior, influenced initially by a strict Protestant rearing, is now existential. Joan is the only woman I *want* to sleep with because I find her physically attractive, because she is the only woman I want to share my person with, and because we are convinced that our children *and* we need the security which that loyalty effects. Joan is committed to me in the same fashion. We communicate easily and enjoy each other's company. I'd rather fight with her than switch—even for a night! This maturing physical attraction, broadening mutuality, and deepening personal loyalty bind us as one. I enjoy being yoked with Joan in matrimony. I love our three children and accept family responsibilities gladly.

I'm not bored with my vocation, marriage, or family. My decision to attack the church stems from my personal disdain for its institutional irrelevance. Like Freud, Russell, and others, I consider that Christianity and the church—having served man at earlier stages in his development—is excess baggage for modern man. No critical mind can accept the pre-Copernican dogmas, outpaced style of life, and communal navel-gazing that *is* the church. I will attack from within. The religious mentality must be liquidated.

Decisively,

Ted

II

THE AFFABLE ENEMY UNMASKED

Every man takes care that his neighbor shall not cheat him. But a day comes when he begins to care that he does not cheat his neighbor. Then all goes well. He has changed his market-cart into a chariot of the sun.

—RALPH WALDO EMERSON

VI

New Canaan
5 March, 1969

Dear Ted,

I shall proceed on the assumption that your decision is firmly made. The strategy of attack is simple. Begin at the top. Discourage, disrupt, and discredit the clerical leadership in your parish. Clergymen are as unevenly competent as other "professionals." The elemental flaws in their "professional" competence are three: like medical doctors, they have a thin education in the humanities; like public school teachers, they exhibit an uncertain exercise of leadership; like scientists and technologists, they have a confused image of their role in society. Expose those flaws, rub them raw—but do not attack your clergy as persons. Many parishioners will rise to their defense; and some clergy, uncertain about what it means to be genuinely human, will react defensively. But there are proven ways to undermine the clerical leadership in any parish. Let me suggest several. They are petty, but it's the snide attacks that cause many concerned clergy to lose heart.

Invite Dr. and Mrs. Jameson to dinner periodically. At fifty-nine, he is getting weary in his work. Play on that. Tell him you don't see how he manages his schedule. Encourage him to feel that his work is more demanding than anyone else's. Persuade him and his wife that they can come to your home anytime to let their hair down. There is a thin line between every man's healthy need for understanding and his unhealthy disposition to neurotic dependency. Coax your minister to cross that line.

Listen carefully to Jameson's sermons and those of his colleagues. Take careful notes as you did in your university classes. Know precisely what your clergy say and why; magnify the tension created by the controversial strands in their preaching by agreeing with those members who take exception to clerical views and by disagreeing with those who support the clergy's objectives. Whenever you're caught in these dissembling activities, reply innocently that you are fostering dialogue in the parish! But don't misquote your clergy. It is more damaging to quote them literally—*out of context*. Americans have become adept at this vicious way of passing judgment on their public officials. Adapt the technique to your parish; teach others to use it. Also, be diligent in carrying tales—"They are saying . . ." But don't identify "they," and decline to be concrete on "that." This will weary your clergy.

Encourage your parson to play "it might have been." Like able men in other professions and in the business community, most competent clergymen would have succeeded in other fields had they entered them. Get your padre to envision the success he might have had in business, law, medicine, or public life. Strong men rarely come single-mindedly to college to study for the ministry. The "call" catches most of them by surprise. What vocational dream claimed Jameson's eager heart in the days of his youth—architecture, law, teaching, politics? Get him to reminisce; he's vulnerable. Many clergymen who dreamed initially of another vocation and set out to prepare for it were dissuaded by a benighted inner constraint to serve the church. Needle Jameson on what might have been.

Sabotage your senior minister's personal appraisal of his effectiveness as a preacher, counselor, and teacher. With an edge of sadness, tell him how your mind rebels and your emotions recoil when his preaching lays bare the lacks in your person. Identify responsible church members who praise him in his presence while boasting at the club and the tavern how they let his preaching roll off like water from a duck's back. When he preaches plainly on practical issues, name those members who express their resentment to others; he knows how few give him any opportunity for dialogue.

Magnify the problems in your denominational church. If you were an Episcopalian you could complain about Malcolm Boyd, Joe Fletcher, or the Anglo-Catholics. If you were a Lutheran you could charge the liberals with undermining Scripture through demythologization and accuse the conservatives of making Scripture irrelevant by trying to confine God to the Bible and dogma. If you were a Methodist you could deplore the confessionless ground on which your church seeks renewal. If you were a member in the United Church of Christ you could insist that social action and gospel preaching are incompatible. If you were a Baptist you could warn raucously against the Protestant drift toward a super-church. But you *are* a United Presbyterian. How fortunate! Your Confession of 1967—often in the public eye during the mid-1960's—can be an effective instrument for subversion, if you use it *cleverly*.[1] Try these gambits for openers: The Confession undermines the Bible. The Confession is a manifesto for the church to get into politics. The Confession threatens our national interests. Attack your new church-school curriculum. Turn an occasional blast on Carson Blake and the World Council of Churches. Swing at the National Council of Churches once in awhile, too.

The staff ministry in your parish also provides opportunity for subversive activity. Direct your attacks against Jameson's *associates*. Twenty-five years ago, the target was the senior minister who "got" assistants at a pittance, used them as errand boys, and at the first sign of their competence, shipped them off to "a larger challenge." Today, most senior ministers recognize the absolute need for competent staff ministries. They choose their ordained associates and lay colleagues because of demonstrated effectiveness and willingness to work. They open full ministries to them, treat them as competent professionals, see to it that they are remunerated generously, and encourage their growth as persons. Consequently, staff members stay five, eight, ten years, and longer. Today's senior in a staff ministry, like an able general, values his staff members as co-workers, likes them personally, and enjoys the camaraderie of a staff ministry. *Protectiveness* is Jameson's point of vulnerability. Complain about his colleagues' inexperience, the length of their sermons, their undisciplined children, their unreasonable demands on church school teachers, their urgent but inexperienced appeals for congregational involvement in the community. These carping criticisms will distress, hurt, and infuriate Jameson; they will disconcert and irritate his colleagues.

Don't disdain the tactics I've suggested. It's not the large-scale battles that exhaust the clergy; it's the day-by-day petty skirmishes that drain them dry. Since pastoral courage awakens lay courage, cut your clergy down to size.

Cordially,

Jim

P.S. Don't write. Just get to work. I'll write again this weekend, offering a few suggestions for undermining your elected lay leaders.

VII

New Canaan
8 March, 1969

Dear Saboteur,

Question your church's use of benevolence monies. That is a good way to stir dissension in the Session. At all levels in the church, discussions on money in general and benevolence in particular are unrealistic, often hypocritical, sometimes dishonest. I have a friend who served for ten years on his denomination's board of world missions. He swears that one of his fellow board members, a well-heeled layman from the South, was a vocal racist. Elected by uncritical churchmen, that man had a voice in administering benevolence monies to Christianize dark-skinned people in Africa and India, while working openly to maintain a segregated congregation in the land of the free! But that *is* the church. The black man's animosity toward the church is understandable.

The real critique of church members on race is not that they participated tardily in the civil rights revolution but that they *are* racist. Officially—since policy statements are cheap—the church appears to be shifting its stance with Fabian haste. But—in spite of involved clergy, high-sounding ecclesiastical declarations, and a rash of paternalistic economic grants—the church remains racist. It has not repented of that sin against God and man. Eleven o'clock every Sunday continues to be the most segregated hour in America. Now, the black churches are going in for segregation, too. Each racial group seeks to perpetuate its own institutions. The institutional church is incurably racist. Industry, sports, entertainment, and education out-distance all religious institutions in placing talent above color.

White congregations depend economically on members who work for companies that assume little initiative in fostering equal employment and open housing and decline to risk their capital in urban renewal ventures. That's not "innocent racism." Furthermore, the church's broad involvement in the racial crisis is blocked by a substantial number of church members—Protestant, Roman Catholic, and Orthodox—who have investments (large and modest) which buttress the present socioeconomic and political structure. That's not "innocent racism." On the other hand, I wonder how many middle-class black church members have an economic stake in this dehumanizing social pattern, too. *Self-interest is color-blind.*

A major reason why more substantial progress has not been made in implementing the 1954 Supreme Court decision on desegregating the public schools is the laissez-faire, and in some places negative, attitude of millions of church members (white and black) in thousands of American communities. Most Americans are willing to recognize civil rights in principle; few are ready to accept the economic (equal employment practices) and social changes (open housing and equal education) necessary to make those rights a reality.[2] "The institutional church inspirits and buttresses this socioeconomic *status quo*. It simply cannot heal itself. You know that. Attack in the name of human decency.

Another thrust in this subversive campaign can center on the church's use of benevolence monies for social ministry. Get at the heart of that "holy" mess without any preliminaries. How can the church—engulfed by rising costs and declining income—maintain homes for the aged, children's homes, hospitals, and adoption agencies in an expanding planned economy? Can the same people contribute twice through tax dollars and church dollars? Many cannot; and those who can—should they? Is this once essential work a proper concern of the church in a welfare state? Does it demonstrate a responsible stewardship of monies and personnel? These questions will anger some of your colleagues because the political implications are unpalatable to them. The questions will confuse others because the Christian implications are ambiguously defined.

But there are other tactics for undermining the elected lay leadership in your parish. Try these.

Study your colleagues on the official board; they are not evenly motivated to serve. Some seek election because they think it's good for business or enhances their reputations as men on the way up in the corporation. Others want the office because their *self*-image requires it: "Jones works selflessly for the church." Some work for the office because they like to play "church" as other men enjoy golf or poker. A mix like that makes subversion easy. Just call for an official endorsement of scattered-site housing!

There are, of course, competent and sincere men and women serving on your church board. A different tactic is required to get at them. Remind them how some fellow board members, resenting *their* leadership, resist and sabotage their ideas. Pour salt on old wounds inflicted by majority votes that were penurious, parochial, petty. Discredit any imaginative proposal that comes up for discussion. Disciplined imagination is rare in our institutions of society; throttle it in the local congregation. That Great Dissenter, Justice Oliver Wendell Holmes, liked to tell about the man who deducted five dollars from his valet's weekly wages "for *lack* of imagination." That temper of mind is sorely lacking in our social institutions today. If Rome went down on "a failure of nerve," Western society may falter because of a failure of imagination.

Be "spiritual" (vacuous) when practical matters are to be decided. If the Session is seeking ways to confront members on their minimal participation in the life of the church, call for "compassion" and suppress truth. When nominees for the Session are discussed as *churchmen* insist that one should not judge his neighbor, ignoring, of course, the historical necessity to make judgments honestly, realistically, and charitably. Be specific. Explain that Smythe can't get to church more than once a month because his legal (or medical) practice requires him to rest on Sundays, but soft-pedal the fact that he attends a steady round of cocktail parties because they provide him with new clients (patients)—and relaxation. Argue that Cotton's extreme right-wing political views qualify him for the board because he will give it balance. Insist that Brown's extreme left-wing views will give the board an avant-garde look. Insist that socially prominent Ritter will add stature to the board even though his chief asset is the thrift of his ancestors. Most board members are eager to prove Jesus' trenchant observation that "the children of this world are in their generation wiser than the children of light." Help them.

Be tightfisted when the issues to be decided are beyond human measurement. Insist that parish membership should be defined on the basis of a member's economic contributions. Complain that the annual apportionment is unfair to your congregation. Suggest that necessary budget increases will, if endorsed by the board, disaffect the general membership. Fuss about the young people's hard use of the church property (scouts, teen hangout, dances, and so forth). Call attention to the sexton's oversights, demanding that he perform like a junior executive while being paid a peon's wage. Dissuade the Session from listening to parishioners who *act* constructively; encourage them to listen to members who simply *react*. Press for simplistic solutions to complex problems. This latter procedure, which almost destroyed a modern political party, will breed chaos in the parish.

Finally, discourage your colleagues from listening to secular voices critical of the church. Keep the talkers in the congregation talking. Encourage the unenlightened enthusiasts to get "where the action is." Muffle the prophetic voices. Discredit the practical leaders. Support programmatic approaches to stewardship, evangelism, and ecumenism. One medieval historian, discussing feudalism, described that historical phenomenon as "confusion roughly organized." Get your parish into that condition and keep it there. The surest way to do that is to guarantee that the blind lead the blind and that the bland lead the bland.

Sincerely,

Jim

P.S. Don't write. Tomorrow's letter will provide suggestions for getting into the woodwork of the congregation!

VIII

New Canaan
9 March, 1969

Dear Ted,

Undermining the congregation is like shooting fish in a rain barrel!

Have a go at the church school. If it isn't already a rival

43

"congregation," make it one. Call for a separate treasury, a superintendent, a full complement of officers, and monthly association meetings. That may create a splinter "congregation" that will compete with the church congregation. Oppose your national church's new curriculum on the ground that it's too advanced for the members in your church. Campaign for simple "Bible stories." Torpedo any effort to set up theological study groups. Stifle informed, candid conversation on social issues. Sabotage every effort directed toward enlisting a competent teaching staff. Oppose sabbaticals for creative teachers; drain them dry. For years the Sunday school hour has been "the most wasted hour in the week." Keep it that way in your church.

Second, most women's auxiliaries are poised for trouble! Generally, the religious outlook of a woman is decidedly subjective. Few women are theologically sophisticated in their Christian witness. Dorothy Sayers, Georgia Harkness, and Barbara Ward are exceptions that prove the rule! Discourage in-depth Bible study; keep the ladies busy with "religious" topics and social activities. And don't overlook their parish housekeeping duties as a field for subversion. The care of the altar, preparation of the communion vessels, direction of fellowship dinners, oversight of coffee hours, and similar tasks are quite mundane but necessary for orderly parish life. Encourage your fellow board members to minimize those services. This will produce a rash of irritating situations that will disrupt parish life and witness. Finally, don't neglect to fan the fires of envy among the ladies. Combustible points are personal appearance, age, husband's success, children's achievements, formal education, social status. Throw verbal matches into these powder kegs and stand clear!

Third, the choirs provide a matchless opportunity for subversion. If Bach were the organist-choirmaster in your parish, some of your members would complain about the music. A tested plan of attack, therefore, can be defined precisely. Follow it to a T.

A. Agree with those members who think the music is too high church and with those who think it is too sentimental. Urge the critics to complain to the chairman of the music committee, the organist, the clergy, and at least three other members after *every* Sunday service.

B. Agree with those members who think the organist-choirmaster demands too much of his volunteer choir and with those who think he sets no musical standards at all. Urge these critics to complain to the chairman of the music committee, the organist, the clergy, and at least three other members after *every* Sunday service.

C. Fight for a single worship service at the sacred hour, 11:00 A.M. If you have an early service (or two), make the worship forms identical with those used at the 11:00 o'clock service. Schedule at least one worship service in competition with the church school hour. Sabotage weekday services—early morning, noon, late afternoon. Oppose responsible experimentation with new forms of worship at unconventional hours on Sunday and on other days of the week.

Don't disdain these petty attacks. It's the petty evils men do in the parish which prevent "the community of faith" from getting on with God's work in the world.

Fourth, youth work in the church offers good terrain for subversive forays. After all, *everyone*—since Socrates first lamented the deterioration of young people in his day— knows that today's youth are headed for perdition. Like all generalizations, this one is destructive; play it to the hilt. It provides a smoke screen for adults who want to avoid facing *their* causative involvement in the rebellion of youth today. It's a dodge against taking earnestly some young people's eloquent questions. Serious young people in Western society *are* wrestling with "gut" issues, which their elders have learned to evade or ignore. Don't provide opportunities for the youth in your parish to speak for themselves; and when they attempt to, frustrate their efforts. Discourage the handful of adult members who want dialogical meetings with youth; engage in double-talk if such meetings occur.

Sabotage every venture in your church and community which allows a few or many teen-agers to confront adults and one another across socioeconomic, racial, and theological lines. Sabotage your clergy's efforts to foster dialogue groups in which youth discuss controversial issues: pacifism, nuclear disarmament, political extremism, psychedelic drugs, abortion, premarital sex, the pill, open housing, social drinking, divorce, capital punishment, mercy killing, organ transplants, and so on. And when any teen-ager in your church gets into trouble —and some will (drugs, sex, demonstrations, riots)—focus self-righteously on the problem rather than compassionately on the person.

Next week I'll suggest some tactics for magnifying the tensions between and among parishes in your community. That's more fun than shooting fish in a rain barrel—and as sporting!

Sincerely,

Jim

IX

Chicago
13 March, 1969

Dear Prof,

You've made your point. Ted Connors is an unconscious subversive. He has been doing haphazardly and ignorantly what you suggested he do systematically and deviously. Ted Connors is the Affable Enemy! I am appalled. Shades of Saul Kane—the harm in being me.

Albert Camus acknowledged sadly that he accepted human duplicity and quit warring against it. I accept that duplicity, too; but I choose to war against it. I agree with Dag Hammarskjöld: "You cannot play with the animal in you without becoming wholly animal, play with falsehood without forfeiting your right to truth, play with cruelty without losing your sensitivity of mind." [3]

Unfortunately, too many laymen, accepting human duplicity (as every man must), quit warring against it. Consequently, their public professions are a mockery because of their private performances. They talk grandly of character and settle meanly for comfort. They sternly urge their children to honor conscience while they boldly seek convenience. They pursue pleasure without responsibility and employ leisure without creative purpose. Consequently, they demonstrate that the church is not in the world so much as the world is in the church. Declining to seek authentic personhood for self and others and pursuing property, power, and prestige (for self, family, class, race, nation), they are—like their unchurched fellow citizens—a people without hope. And I have been one of them.

I intend to remain in the church. I aim to take Christ and man seriously.

Your letters on subversion were written by a skillful teacher. You exposed my destructive churchmanship in short order. At the same time, you recognized my underlying desire to remain in the church and honored my freedom to decide that issue for myself. I'm grateful. But, I'm also puzzled. You know congregational life so well. You have a deft feel for its unsteady pulse. You betray a charitable view on the church. Is it possible that you—a vigorous disciple of the Enlightenment—have joined the ranks of the Christians?

Don't write. I'll be in New York week after next. I've arranged for three days' vacation—the twenty-sixth to the twenty-eighth. I plan to visit the University. I realize that I can't "go home again," but I do want to talk with you at length. Please set the time.

Expectantly,

Ted

X

Chicago
2 April, 1969

Dear Prof,

You turncoat! You fraud! You irrepressible teacher! You, a church member—and an Episcopalian at that! No wonder you wrote so knowledgeably about parish life.

But why didn't you speak of your conversion when I wrote my first letter? When you did tell me about it in the quiet of your study, I was deeply moved. So was Joan when I recounted it to her. Would you provide a firsthand account for her? We feel that we could benefit through a continued correspondence with you on these and related questions. You can provide helpful insights that will contribute to our understanding and practice of the Faith. And your experiences as a vestryman will be enlightening to me as a member of our Session.

Thanks for the hospitality of your home and the meaningful conversations. Anne has grown more charming over the years. She's the ideal wife for a hardheaded, softhearted intellectual like you. Unfortunately, too many people are softheaded and hardhearted these days. You, sir, are indeed "a man for all seasons." I'm indebted to you.

Cordially,

Ted

III

ONE MAN'S CONVERSION

About two thousand years ago, at what we call the beginning of our era, a bunch of Jews were going around Palestine saying the most outlandish thing: that a naked man hung on a gibbet was the true focus of religious faith and liturgy. For such a brutal conjunction of the horribly human and the worshipful, there was and still is absolutely no precedent in the religious history of man. There is no religious category into which it can fit. Relative to man's common religious ideas, it is simply an outrage. One of them, Paul by name, states this fact bluntly. He said that what they were offering was a skandalon (a fatal obstacle to faith) to the religiously well brought up Jews and to the religiously undisciplined Greeks. Jew and Greek between them coveted the whole range of human attitudes at that time, and for both the man-on-the-cross was an outrage. And although this thing they were preaching had no religious category into which it could be fitted and understood, these men had the effrontery to say that it was the fulfillment of all the religious ideas man had ever had.[1]

—DOM SEBASTIAN MOORE

XI

New Canaan
10 April, 1969

Dear Ted,

Anne and I enjoyed your visit immensely; you're an exciting house guest. It's gratifying to know that the conversations were meaningful. Here's a recap of my contributions to them. I hope it proves to be as helpful as you expect.

First, your angry letter against the church distressed me. I felt vaguely responsible. My immediate reaction was to phone, sympathize with you, tell you about my new life as a Christian, persuade you to remain in the church, and urge you to re-examine and test God's demands and promises. On second thought, I decided that approach was patronizing and academic. The subversion bit appealed to me as one way to get *you* to face your casual involvement in the church. You recognized yourself as the Affable Enemy—as most laymen can when confronted with an exaggerated description of contemporary parish life.

Now—my conversion. Everyman, I think, has two religions. The first he inherits from his parents, teachers, peers. It is part of his cultural heritage. The second religion he forges for himself. It is existential and historical. Eventually, the two are alike, unalike, or a composite. My inherited religion couldn't weather the intellectual critiques at college *and* my debilitating experiences in World War II. The God of my boyhood was scorned at college, wounded on Omaha Beach, gassed at Dachau, and buried in the rubble of Berlin. That "god" was dead, and I didn't mourn his passing. It didn't occur to me then that if the *real* God could be killed by violence, he would have expired in the Roman arena! Unencumbered by any cultural god, I relished my "freedom." But I was not tempted to settle for a meaningless existence—a pervasive mood in Berlin during that desperate winter of 1945-46. After all, *I* had hope! The Army provided for *my* physical needs. Loving Anne and counting the days until *I* would be with her, *I* had no reason to view life as absurd. The sociopolitical debacle in Europe was not only explainable but open to rectification. That was my judgment on the situation. I was convinced that social man's hope lay in the law—conceived imaginatively, administered wisely, and supported by a citizen-controlled exercise of force. Humane laws—realistically framed and imaginatively administered—I concluded, are man's chief bulwark against his inhumanities to his fellows. During my graduate study for the Ph.D. in political science, those judgments became firm. The year you enrolled in my courses in political science and government, I had just been promoted to an associate professorship. Pleased with myself and with life, I had hit full stride in my attacks on the church, lackluster public education, and unimaginative hacks in career politics. You got the brunt of that brittle thinking, and I kept at it for another decade.

In December, 1960—five days before Christmas—Anne was involved in a four-car collision on the Parkway. The hospital notified me that she had been seriously injured. I rushed there, imagining the worst, hoping for the best, but making no plea to God. Anne's injuries were serious indeed. She hovered between life and death for eleven days and was hospitalized for five and a half months. Those eleven days were hell; the five months shook my foundations. My wife and I had had a meaningful marriage and an exciting home from the beginning; the children and I missed her desperately.

When Anne was off the critical list, I continued to visit her daily. I met her minister frequently. Our meetings were pleasant, but I kept him at arm's length. Anne had worshiped regularly in the Episcopal Church during the years of our marriage. She had been confirmed after I shipped out for North Africa in early 1942. Although I had attended services with her at the military base where we lived before I went overseas, I did not attend church after returning to the States.

Anne had been a graduate student in English literature when I met her at school. We fell madly in love and married within ten weeks! During my four plus years overseas, she completed her master's degree and taught in a high school in Baltimore. Her daily letters were compassionate, intelligent, and good-humored. Eighty percent of those letters reached me, sometimes a dozen at a time. I, too, wrote often and openheartedly. Doors of understanding opened between us. I conversed candidly with her on every subject except religion, ignoring that strand in her correspondence. When I returned to the States we were well along in knowing each other as persons. Accepting her membership in the church, I declined to press her with my rejection of her God. When, over the years, our three children were baptized—which I agreed to because Anne wanted it—I was not present. Her parents were the sponsors.

In the first years after my return from Europe, the question of the church came up frequently because Anne introduced it. She presented intelligibly the basic Christian teachings but said little about her experience of God. I listened but never dialogued. I honored her freedom to decide as she wanted, and she honored mine. Aware that she loved her Episcopal church, I thought she "loved" it without being seriously involved in Christianity. After all, many church members are devoted to the church without getting involved with Christ and other persons. I was discovering that my wife was not one of those people.

Anne's gallantry in the face of physical suffering and her handling of the separation from the children and me was magnificent. I had expected her to require comfort and support from me and the children. Accepting both appreciatively, she didn't really need either. That surprised and deflated me. When I recognized that she was comforting *me*—literally, making *me* strong—my ego was wounded. Brooding on that for a week or so, I finally suggested that females are fashioned to be sturdy and compassionate and that she was, after all, the ideal female! She ignored my facile observation, turning the conversation into other channels. Before I bid her goodnight, however, she insisted quietly that her faith in Christ undergirded the stability and produced the serenity I had perceived. She asked me to pray with her. I stated flatly that I would not. Irritated, I charged her with violating my freedom. Meanly, I accused her of being disloyal to me. She cried, hard, for only the second time in our married life. Our parting was severely strained.

I didn't pray that night. I didn't sleep soundly either. Tossing, and turning, I smoked and fretted and brooded. Did Anne really believe that mythical nonsense (as I viewed it then)? Or, was she a long-term victim of cultural conditioning by the church? Twenty-two years of marriage had revealed her to me as an intellectually gifted, wholesome, cultured woman—a fascinating companion, an exciting love-partner, a devoted mother, a critical colleague, an informed and involved citizen. Surely, her "Christian testimony" would diminish after her recovery. On that sanguine judgment, I fell into a fitful sleep. I dreamed of death and skeletons dancing in the streets—having read again, several nights before, J. Huizinga's matchless work, *The Waning of the Middle Ages!* [2] Next morning, disturbed by my bizarre dreams, I assured myself nonetheless that they were not linked to my unwillingness to face death existentially nor rooted in my stubborn refusal to consider whether Anne's God gets involved with persons.

Several days later, I asked my wife if she received help from her minister's visits. She said she did. I asked if she believed in the immanence of God. She said she did. I asked if she experienced the presence of Christ. She said she did. I asked if she believed in the resurrection. She said she did. Plainly, one facet of her person was outside my ken—and had been for years. I made an appointment with a professor in the school of theology here at the University, described my situation, acknowledged my confusion, confessed my resentment, and expressed my concern. He was so damned academic about my problem, I didn't get any help at all. After brooding another week or so, I decided to read the Gospels critically—to exorcise my demon, Anne's god.

I set out to read the Gospels with the mind I called for in my students when they were required to read political documents like the Magna Charta, the Bill of Rights, Lincoln's Second Inaugural—read as though one were meeting the ideas and the framing of them for the *first time*. I read the Revised Version of the Gospels at one sitting, not understanding much, yet sensing that something significant was happening to *me*. I was attracted, but not persuaded. I discovered eventually that Scripture, unlike dogma, is *personal*—existential as well as historical.

From a single *critical* reading of the Gospels I recognized that the God presented in those documents of faith and fact was not the God I had rejected years before. According to the evangelists, Jesus was a man so authentically human that they accepted him as God in human form *and* staked their lives on that objective-subjective judgment. They remembered him as the Man who healed broken bodies, restored sight, forgave sin, met evil head-on, allowed self-righteous religionists and self-seeking politicians to kill him, endured his crucifixion courageously and confidently, was raised from the dead as he had promised, and created a new community in which men were enabled to become truly human by accepting him and revealing him to others through loving deeds and words of personal witness. His chroniclers presented all this and their experiences with him as historical events. Disciplined to be critical-minded, I admitted that this was the first time I had examined the source documents on Christianity. Conditioned to be pragmatic, I admitted that I had never tested the validity of the Christian message. I decided to risk study and experimentation.

I began to attend worship services after an absence of years, taking the step three months before Anne returned from the hospital. Attending her Episcopal Church, I was attracted at once by the liturgy and the sermons. My youthful experience had been in a rural congregation of another denomination served by an uncultured preacher who told the old, old story in sermon after sermon without any evident knowledge of man's ambivalent nature, the ambiguities of his historical situation, or the power of the gospel to transform human life *now*. This superficial, banal recital was carried on in a barren, unaesthetic setting. My experience was flat, dull, unreal.

My response to the Episcopal liturgy was affirmative. The congregational-personal confession of sin in the Book of Common Prayer appealed strongly to me. One declaration especially caught my critical attention: "There is no health in us." That description of man thrust me back to war-ravished Germany. It spoke to *me*. I had inspected Dachau; its indescribable horrors still haunt me. But I had never probed at the root causes of those inhumanities. For the first time in my life, it occurred to me that Watts, Rochester, Newark, Detroit, and Dallas, Texas, in November, 1963—and so many *family* situations every day of every year—are the quintessence of Dachau.

Man, coveting power, emasculates Truth, corrupts justice, strangles compassion. In the Nazi State, a German gentile possessed power that a German Jew lacked. In New Haven—and in Detroit, Memphis, and Los Angeles—an American white possesses power that an American black does not command. A man of economic means possesses power denied a poor man. It is this human lust for power which makes love essential if people are to treat others as persons, not pawns. It also makes democratic laws an absolute necessity. In subsequent readings, I discovered that Reinhold Niebuhr, years before, had put my then-emerging thoughts into a succinct sentence: "Man's capacity for justice makes democracy possible; but man's inclination to injustice makes democracy necessary." [3] And if power corrupts and absolute power corrupts absolutely, as Lord Acton observed, then every social problem roots in the *nature* of man himself.[4] Evil is always personal *and* sociological; but it is never *merely* sociological. Collective forces are at work in society, but, conscious or unconscious, they root in human nature. That was my new conclusion. After all, who can claim honestly that he fully understands another man's ambivalent nature *or* his own? If holistic understanding is to come, I reasoned, it must be "given" by Someone outside man, experienced in all man's infirmities, yet able to overmatch the inherent limitations in humanity.

From the first service I attended, listening critically and participating thoughtfully, the epistle and Gospel lessons also spoke to me. Singing the hymns, I was surprised how frequently a line or verse would stir my thoughts: "Greater good because of evil . . . " That made sense, I concluded, if one accepts the Cross as God's efficacious deed. The sermons broke in on me immediately. The preacher was declaring an Event and interpreting and demonstrating its meaning for contemporary man. I perceived that the educated, cultured man in the pulpit *believed,* as Anne *believed,* in Jesus Christ. I realized that the bond between Anne and her minister and between them and others in the church was Christ. Accepting him, they accepted each other as persons. Their mutual trust in him produced a community of persons.

But a sense of community is not unique to Christians. I had experienced it at the University with persons who love ideas and work to communicate them to students, and with students who pursue learning. I had recognized long ago that man commits himself to someone or something—creative, destructive, inane—and that his commitment establishes a community between and among persons similarly committed. I also knew that every man has his god (s). I had fought Hitler's Supermen; I had schemed eighteen hours a day to outwit the Russians in Berlin; both enemies gave primary allegiance to the state. But which god, if any, is able to lift man to a higher humanity? Could it be this Christ? I had to *explore* that possibility or admit intellectual bias (perverse willfulness). No avenue of honorable retreat remained open to me.

After Anne came home we talked endlessly—she calmly and happily and I argumentatively and irritably. I was desperately afraid of being taken in. I accused her angrily one day of being overly emotional about everything. I told her that she "felt" too much and that people who "feel" too much can't think soundly. Her response struck home: "People who can't feel deeply simply aren't truly human."

Eventually, I made an appointment with Anne's priest, Dr. Conrad. I was comfortable with him from the beginning. He wasn't academic, argumentative, or apologetic for his faith. He told me what he believed and why. He admitted candidly to doubts. He reminded me that each man decides for himself whether he will accept Christ's Lordship. He reasoned persuasively that each makes or declines to make Kierkegaard's "leap of faith." [5] He also argued cogently that Christians do not follow "cunningly devised fables," that faith in Christ is not blind choice.

We also discussed the reliability of the record of God's deeds in history (Bible), the significance of dogmas as confessions of faith by particular Christians in particular eras of history, and the changing life-style of the Christian community (church) across the centuries. Dr. Conrad helped me to recognize that revelation is a continuing activity of God; that man can have the institutional church without Christ but he cannot have Christ apart from his church.[6] At his suggestion, I read, among others, Alan Richardson's *New Testament Literature,* R. B. Scott's *Relevance of the Prophets,* J. S. Whale's *Christian Doctrine,* Reinhold Niebuhr's *Children of Light and the Children of Darkness,* D. Bonhoeffer's *The Cost of Discipleship,* and R. Bultmann's *Jesus and the Word.* I read and conversed, quibbled and quarreled, studied and meditated—and decided. After formal instruction in the Faith, the Bishop confirmed me in April, 1962.

Sincerely,

Jim

XII

Chicago
27 April, 1969

Dear Prof,

Joan was moved by the account of your conversion. We've talked for hours about a dimension of life that we have rarely spoken of since our days at the University. Suddenly, life is richer, more mysterious; it's taken on a new dimension.

But we get bogged down on questions like these. Why did you decide for Christ while Albert Camus decided to go it alone? Did you, a child of the Enlightenment, suspend reason at some point to become a Christian? Must an intellectual prostitute reason to make the "leap of faith"? Was Camus more honest intellectually than you and I? Why do so many of my educated contemporaries ignore the church or unite with it casually for the sake of family solidarity and community acceptance? What significant difference has Christianity made in *your* life?

We tackled some of these questions when I visited with you two months ago, but another go at them will suggest some guidelines for Joan and me in our discussion and study.

Gratefully,

Ted

XIII

New Canaan
10 May, 1969

Dear Ted,

Why did conversion happen to me? My experience can be illuminated by rational observations, but it defies any neat rationale. Unquestionably, Anne's accident triggered it. Exercising my freedom, I made a series of personal responses to that and subsequent events. After a season of antagonistic evasion I *decided* to examine the Gospels critically, worship regularly, converse with Christians, expose myself to the church's formal instruction, and unite with the believers in a particular tradition of the Faith, the Episcopal Church. I have since endeavored to act on my growing Christian knowledge and insights. I still have doubts; indeed, they are more complex now than when I lived outside the Christian Faith. Doubt and faith are, in reality, inseparable. Otherwise, faith would be servitude.

Actually, doubts that stem from one's honest desire to experience reality can be as sacred as worship itself. Such doubts are indispensable to the birth of faith. But the birth of faith is not the death of doubt. Doubts that stem from one's continuing desire to experience reality are essential to the maturing of faith. Paul was "perplexed (doubtful) but not driven to despair." Jesus questioned the necessity of drinking the cup, even as he accepted it in trust. To wait for an ultimate solution to *any* problem before one accepts Christ is not to accept him at all. Emotionally healthy people do not approach marriage, parenting, business, a profession, or politics

63

that way. Doubt, uncertainty, and perplexity are strands in every authentic life experience. The *only* doubt inconsistent with the Christian Faith is the doubt that Paul Tillich calls "total doubt"—the suspension of the option of deciding and acting on the demands of Christ.

Over the last decade I've read extensively in church history and in the history of ancient and medieval civilizations. Reading Bainton, Latourette, and Butterfield has convinced me that educated Christians will witness more effectively if they study some good Christian biography and a sound general history of Christianity. Historical inquiry reveals that (a) the Faith empirically establishes itself; (b) the Faith enables men to make some sense of many complex events in life; (c) the Faith enables man to become authentically human.

The Jews and Gentiles in the first Christian century had a world view that was radically different from our own. Their socioeconomic-technological-political orientation and patterns of life were essentially different from ours. But they faced the same elemental problems of human existence that we face: personal insecurity and alienation, the struggle for identity, a firm ground for hope, a faith to live by. Today, concerned churchmen and educators are getting so preoccupied with the kaleidoscopic changes in our society that they gloss over the elemental concerns of human existence. Openness to change is necessary to life. I agree with the late John Kennedy, who said in an address at Yale University in 1962: "Too often we hold fast to the clichés of our forebears. We subject all facts to a prefabricated set of interpretations. We enjoy the comfort of opinion without the discomfort of thought." [7] Leaders in all fields need to be challenged to appraise the tempo, likely direction, and possible impact of contemporary changes on persons and institutions.

64

But preoccupation with an unknowable future numbs man's capacity to decide and act on the evidence at hand. To halt indefinitely before decisions that *must* be made is enervating to persons and demoralizing to institutions. Jacques Barzun has pointed out this condition in the academic community. "We sit and wait for the reports to tell us what to do, and our self-consciousness grows faster than our knowledge or our will. Only our faith in progress, our faith in the automatism of our methods and our gadgets, keep us in countenance. The paradox here is that turning the academic experts loose on the so-called problems of society tends toward the general paralysis. The mania for analyzing and investigating is one form of well-recognized disorder known in psychiatry by the French name of *folie du doute.* The cure for the disease is obviously a philosophic review of means and ends. But the attempt would require detachment, a proper measure of idleness, and a liberal, as against a *professional,* outlook. And . . . these are the very attributes excluded by the modern design and impetus of the university." [8]

The current trend in the church is to talk more and more about change, but to affirm less and less the changeless; to analyze and diagnose endlessly but to act rarely, and then cautiously and hesitantly. For two centuries the Western world has been sliding into ethical nihilism; for two decades it has been rushing into it. That tide can be checked only by authentic affirmations cast in relevant forms and acted on boldly in the interests of persons. Relevance is assured wherever the church is faithful in word and deed to basic biblical affirmations.

Currently, the church is too tentative on affirming God-in-Christ (Event). It is too eager to fondle each little nuance of what is happening institutionally, too inclined to have faith in

65

"faith" (religious, scientific, and so on), too disposed to talk about "love as the only norm." [9] The church—first rationalizing faith in revealed religion and then losing confidence in reason and finally declining to respect principles—is now given to minimizing objective reality and maximizing subjective experience. The issue is not *who* one believes in and *what* one does, but *whether* one believes and does. Everyone is encouraged "to do his thing" whatever that might be! When churchmen—Protestant and Roman Catholic—show more zeal for open inquiry into the relevance of Christ than for knowing the person and nature and work of Christ and more interest in the "honesty" part of the equation, "honesty in the church," than in the "church" part, a serious loss of Christian faith has occurred.[10] The church must update its dogmas and adapt its institutional forms if it is to dialogue meaningfully and serve effectively in today's world. It must be true to the gospel if it is to *serve God in the world*. A theological frame of reference *is* essential if social-political action is to be Christian.

The twentieth-century world is not yesterday's world, but its *roots* are in yesterday's world. Galileo, Newton, and Fermi provided new balconies on the world of nature. Marx and Freud provided new orientations on the nature of society and man. Kierkegaard, Heidegger, and Sartre provided fresh insights on man's need to be human. These orientations enlarge man's freedom to choose the stance from which he will meet life. But there is nothing absolute or sacred about the Hegelian view of Spirit, the Freudian view of man, the Marxist thesis of dialectical materialism, the democratic experiment, or Sartre's existential pessimism. Each rests on a human *theory* formulated by fallible human beings. Each theory can be examined and tested. The biblical view, on the other hand, claims to rest on revelation—God's purposeful participation in history. That view can be examined and tested, too. The choice is open to everyone. When John's disciples asked Jesus if they should report that he was the Christ, he told them to relate what they saw him doing and John could decide that for himself.

Widespread rejection of rigid dogmas built on a pre-Copernican view of the universe, a pre-Freudian view of man, and a static moral philosophy was inevitable in this era of science and technology. Critical scientists and impatient existentialists have enlarged the church's freedom to witness. But some scientists and existentialists reject *all* Scripture and *all* tradition on purely subjective grounds. Camus, for example, judging whether God gives meaning to life, declared that "there is no choice, and that is where the bitterness comes in." The fallacy of his argument is in his contention that *"there is no choice."* Dismissing the experiences of Paul and Augustine, Luther and Wesley, Bonhoeffer and John XXIII—and the thousands of millions of believers over nineteen centuries—Camus insisted that *his* experience is the *only* valid criterion for accepting or rejecting the nature of God and man. That is subjectivity raised to the nth power. On *this* judgment, Camus reminds me of a colleague in my department—twice married, twice divorced—who insists that *my* marital happiness is an illusion because *he* has had two bad experiences! It is the height of subjectivity to conclude that those who experience the presence of God are illusionists because others experience the absence of God.

But faith cannot be forced. Certainly, learning does not come by coercion or simply by indoctrination. Professors discover quickly that "you can lead a boy to college, but you can't make him think." Parents realize that a child's love cannot be coerced. So faith cannot be forced. The case for it can be argued rationally—up to a point. It can be presented empirically—up to a point. But the *freedom* to believe, like the freedom to disbelieve, is every man's option. Each person decides whether he will be a nihilist, an agnostic, a humanist, a Buddhist, or a Christian. Nietzsche, convinced that God was dead and that the church was his monument, urged man to believe in man, become superman, be his own god. In that plea, the brilliant German philosopher was logically consistent. Without faith in someone or something man ceases to be *man*.

I am not devaluating reason. I prize it more highly now than I did in my pre-Christian years. In one sense, I agree with Thomas Aquinas who argued that it is immoral to believe in Christ if one's reason does not condone one's doing so. Jesus, valuing human reason, appealed to it vigorously. In another sense, however, I reject Aquinas' judgment that faith and reason are wholly reconcilable. The heart does entertain reasons that reason does not understand. And Jesus appealed openly to man's emotions: "Lovest thou me?" Further, he challenged each human being to exercise his personal freedom to choose: "Test the doctrine." But he also admitted that mystery and ambiguity are strands in life: "No man knows the hour . . ." Christ confronts the whole man in the context of time *and* eternity. The Christian Faith involves intellectual assent, emotional involvement, volitional commitment, obedience, and trust. It is not static; it is dynamic. Christian Faith examines and tests its working premises regularly, adapting them to fresh insights into God, man, and the world. But unless it accepts Christ as Lord and acts on his demands, it is not Christian Faith.

Since my conversion, my life appears to be as it was before I got involved with Christ in and through his Church. After all, the Christian life is not out of this world, but in it. How could it be otherwise? I continue to serve as a professor in a thoroughly secular university, to be happily married, to be a concerned parent, and to serve in community affairs. But there is a qualitative difference in my person. Consequently, there is a qualitative difference in my familial and communal relationships. My style of life has been altered radically.

I do not ask, "What would Jesus do?" That would deny my freedom to be truly human. Instead, I seek to discern the mind of Christ and to decide issues in the light of his mind in me. Christianity rejects any rigid conformity to fixed patterns —even his. Dostoevsky, in his creative novel *The Brothers Karamazov,* has the Grand Inquisitor say to the Prisoner (Christ): "In place of rigid ancient law, man must hereafter with free heart decide for himself what is good and what is evil, having only Thy image before him as his guide." [11] Christianity does not provide neat answers to complex human problems or gloss over life's ambiguities.

Man is created for fellowship with God *and* with other men. He is restless, fragmented, alienated from others until he accepts God's gift of new life through Christ. That, I think, is what Tertullian meant when he said that man is *naturally* Christian. Man is created to be authentically human. Redemption is God's means of restoring what he created and man emasculated—true humanity. Real life has two focuses— fidelity to God and fidelity to humanity. They meet in Christ.

Fraternally,

Jim

P.S. *Please* do drop the "Prof" salutation.

IV

IN SEARCH OF NEW VALUES

Jesus' "lack of moral principles." He sat at meat with publicans and sinners, he consorted with harlots. Did he do this to obtain their votes? Or did he think that, perhaps, he could convert them by such "appeasement"? Or was his humanity rich and deep enough to make contact, even in them, with that in human nature which is common to all men, indestructible, and upon which the future has to be built? [1]

—DAG HAMMARSKJÖLD

XIV

Dear Prof,

I've been troubleshooting at our overseas plants and distribution centers. I have read your last letter a half dozen times. It is in my briefcase now. I get your points clearly.

God-in-Christ came "eyeball to eyeball" with man so that man can see who he was created to be and how the restoration of his authentic humanity can be accomplished. That rugged confrontation was costly to God. It is also costly to man. There is no "cheap grace."

Unfortunately, my generation avoids confrontation and shuns sacrifice. A distorted view of democracy and a worshipful attitude toward technology combine to make us subservient to consensus judgments and manipulative skills. Gauging the value of persons on the basis of their "personal" acceptability and their "usefulness," managing institutions efficiently, and manipulating machines expertly, we conclude uncritically that the same value judgments, methods, and techniques work in *all* human relations. And they do, superficially; but in "working" they maim the manipulator and the manipulated.[2]

Of course, the disposition to manage situations *and* the disposition to manipulate and coerce persons in order to control them is as old as man. Jacob defrauded Esau by manipulating Isaac. The Renaissance Popes were artful manipulators. The Reformers were mercilessly coercive on occasion. Manipulation in all fields of endeavor (politics, business, love-making, parenting) is symptomatic of man's ego-driven, fragmented nature; its dark history is as old as man. But manipulation has become frightfully dangerous in our day because technology has expanded the means for it, and our affluent society rewards those who are good at it. To be saved from it is our desperate need. I should know.

During the past few months I've waded into the new theology literature. It reads quickly. Dr. Jameson and his associates, guiding me, react to the literature on three different levels. Jameson, a kissin' cousin to the new breed theologian all his life, takes the literature in easy stride. His preaching, oriented to historical and existential biblical scholarship, almost kept me from joining Overlook Church years ago. A restrained demythologizer, he jarred my literalist faith! Initially, it was his sensitive social consciousness and personal courage that appealed to me; it still does. In fact, it was my belated recognition of our *congregation's* lethargic response to his preaching, as well as my widening involvement with non-church groups on housing and employment, that precipitated my short-lived rebellion against the church. What I'm getting at is that Jameson—while appreciating Fletcher, Robinson, and Cox—underestimates their contribution to laymen like me. His associates, on the other hand, read the literature voraciously and press it indiscriminately on the laity. One, given his head, would have our parish involved on every social front in Greater Chicago! He sees the new theology as a charter for action. I agree with many of his views, but he frequently gets the cart before the horse. Jameson's other associate, a sensitive traditionalist, is overly suspicious of new forms and cautious on social action. He views the new theology as religious humanism. The associates are good for each other, the parish, and Jameson. I am indebted to all three men for sharing their knowledge, insights, and convictions with me. But you can help me, too.

What are your views on worship and witness? Is there a dynamic relationship between the two? Can one vitally exist apart from the other? Traditionally, United Presbyterians have given priority to the preaching-teaching ministry. Your church, I think, has concentrated on liturgy and the holy communion. Our associates, arguing from opposite poles, have stirred my interest in the worship-witness issue.

Second, please compile a short bibliography of works that enlightened you. But keep in mind that I can't spend thirty hours a week digging into theological and biblical literature! I'm not a graduate student at the University. I'm paid to sell farm machinery. My corporation is not in business to build the Good Society. And my "secular city" of Chicago is no closer to being the kingdom of God today than it was sixty years ago when Upton Sinclair wrote his muckraking novel, *The Jungle*. Galbraith and Cox are *too* intellectual to be practical. They are theorists.

As ever,

Ted

XV

Cambridge, England
28 August, 1969

Dear Ted,

Lecturing at this venerable seat of learning this summer, I am particularly sensitive to the note of pique in your last letter. Stop patronizing the intellectuals. I don't expect your corporation, or any corporation, to use half its profits to rebuild our society; but I do expect you and your associates to *lead* in renewing our urban communities. You should be the catalytic agents that initiate salutary change. Further, I don't celebrate God in the ambiguities of the "secular city" any more readily than I celebrate him in the ambiguities of "the stained-glass jungle." Social critics like Galbraith serve the common-weal because they challenge the American businessman's ingrained disposition to ignore the intellectual and emotional needs of man. You chaps rarely see man as more than a consumer. Business has contributed incalculably to the affluent society; it has done little to fashion the good society. Galbraith points to a basic cause of society's malaise: "The myopic preoccupation with production and material investment has diverted our attention from the more urgent questions of how we are employing our resources and, in particular, from the greater need and opportunity for investing in persons." [3] Needfully, Cox exposes the American churchman's disposition to compartmentalize religion.[4] Many churchmen, finding it safer to administer the institution, do shy away from risking either their person or institution in meeting social issues frontally and getting involved with persons in concrete situations.

Unless creative tension exists between the doers and the thinkers in a complex society, life in that society goes stale or erupts in revolution. That lusty old despot, Catherine the Great of Russia, discussing her reluctance to initiate political reforms, complained to the Encyclopedist Diderot: "You only write on paper but I have to write on human skin, which is incomparably more irritable and ticklish." [5] After weathering a violent revolt of the serfs under Pugachev and brooding over the fate of her unseated predecessors, Catherine stopped trying to "write on human skins." Her decision contributed to the 1917 Revolution in Russia.

Since the days of Catherine and Pugachev, the locus of revolution has shifted from the rural areas to the urban centers, but my argument remains valid. Unless there is creative tension between the thinkers and activists—and unless both thought and action characterize the institutional decision-makers—society explodes or decays. The Industrial Revolution transformed Europe's agrarian society of the Middle Ages and America's rural society of the eighteenth century into an urban culture in the Western world. Business contributed magnificently to the rise of the city. But it has done little for the city in Western society. It has been parasitic. Perceptive social critics have attacked this social problem for decades. Our government has addressed it with rising concern since 1900. Presently, voices of protest are raised in every corner of our nation. The Report of President Johnson's Commission on Civil Disorder is a striking case in point. Martin Luther King dramatized the crucial need to bring the promise of new life to persons in the city. John Lindsay, LeRoi Jones, Daniel Moynihan, Floyd McKissick, Edmund Muskie, Carl Stokes, and thousands more are addressing that need now. Meantime, the business community still lags in facing the urban crisis.

Platoons of business leaders must ally themselves with imaginative leaders in government, education, and the church in a massive cooperative effort to renew the urban centers. Otherwise, a third of this nation will go to pieces under de-humanizing social forces, and that "other America" will be the land of the imprisoned. In fact, since all who live beyond the boundaries of our urban complexes are dominated by urban politics, commerce, and culture, *every* American citizen will be impoverished and millions will be maimed by our mutual unwillingness to fashion a humane society. Unquestionably, the city is the *symbol* of social salvation in this generation.

Business leaders have a social and moral responsibility to renew urban society. They also have an economic stake in the task. Enlightened self-interest should motivate them if nothing else does. National self-interest should motivate our whole citizenry. Riots in urban centers are symptomatic of the social ills in our industrial urban society. A British journalist, commenting on the Watts riot, made this sound historical judgment. "It is not just an American tragedy. . . . What happened in Los Angeles is pretty certainly going to happen in many other countries, both capitalist and communist, as the conditions that caused it spread to them. This was an American phenomenon only in the sense that the United States is half a generation ahead of the rest of the world in the development of an industrial urban society with the special problems that brings. It has the first taste of both the pleasures and the terrors of this new sort of life. . . . It was an insurrection of anarchy, an outburst against any kind of system by the people left at the bottom." [6]

The tardy, but widening involvement of governmental, academic, business, and ecclesiastical personnel in addressing social problems is a sign of hope. Don't cut yourself off from this renaissance.

Cordially,

Jim

XVI

Chicago
10 September, 1969

Dear Prof,

O.K. So, business leaders *have* been slow in facing the urban crisis. Who hasn't? Our politicians talk more boldly than they act. Churchmen discuss the crisis and provide patronizing economic grants rather than tackle its root causes. And *you* academics analyze the urban problem more vigorously than you address it. In fact, the academic community resists necessary changes in its *own* bailiwick until it is shotgunned. The Cox Commission, appointed to study the insurrection at Columbia University, charged not only President Grayson Kirk and the Trustees but the faculty, too, as bearing heavy responsibility for that debacle: "The faculty as a body and most of its members as individuals failed to speak out upon matters of intense student concern." [7]

Of course, the failure of others to be creative architects of a humane society doesn't excuse us businessmen for our cautious, calculated, tentative efforts. The awful truth is that our American citizenry hasn't matured to the point where it can handle democracy in an industrial-urban society, and it is a rare political leader who has the imagination and guts to challenge our citizenry.

Cordially,

Ted

P.S. Where are those observations on worship and witness? Professors do procrastinate!

XVII

New Canaan
20 September, 1969

Dear Ted,

You remind me of that fabulous former light-heavyweight champion, Archie Moore; the harder he was hit the more skillfully he fought back!

You are dead right in your charge. Segments in our college and university faculties, like those who administer the institutions, have contributed to student unrest and revolt because their concern for persons is small and their competence, outside a specialty, is limited. Many of the ablest teachers no longer teach; they prefer to write, do research, or accept administrative posts. Further, the unbridled individualism of *most* professors has militated against a collective faculty voice at our institutions of higher learning. Too many professors view their academic institution as so many devout people view the church: an exclusive club for *their* kind of people and a vehicle for *their* ideas. Both the church and the university prove that "the worst is a corruption of the best."

However, student unrest, like unrest in the church, is directed not only against the university and the church, but against modern society itself. The "system" is under attack. Furthermore, revolts have been part of the history of the university since the middle ages. Reform is also a vigorous strand in church history. Both institutions, at their best, question popular truth; they criticize and prod society when its logic gets out of touch with reality. After all, the Reformation was sparked by a professor's ninety-five Theses at the University of Wittenberg. The current revolt among Roman Catholic priests and bishops is a contemporary case in point. Unrest in the university *and* the church points up the need for reform in both institutions; it also points up the need for reform in society itself.

Now for your question on the relation between witness and worship. Currently, there are churchmen who belittle worship (and preaching) and beat the drums for social action. They make the headlines. But the majority—preoccupied with worship (liturgy, music, architecture)—still avoid social issues. Most congregations and all denominations have both camps. But neither group can call up a single biblical precedent to support its position. Among the early Christians, worship and witness were *inseparable* strands in the Faith. Scripture is plain on that. The people who worshiped in the catacombs of Rome died in the Roman arena. But our discussion will be more fruitful, I think, if we begin with the church situation today rather than with the first, second, and third generation Christians.

By mid-twentieth century, worship in the American church had become esoteric or perfunctory. Evangelism was a program for "getting" church members; stewardship was a device for raising an annual budget; service to man ("social ministry") was either romanticized or institutionalized. The social turbulence of the 1960's; the hit-and-run tactics of the popular parish critics; radical changes in the moral climate of Western society; and new ethical questions prompted by nuclear weapons, electronic inventions, space travel, the urban crisis, organ transplants, and the pill forced many churchmen to examine how far their materially thriving but socially irrelevant institution had deviated from the biblical image of the church: a people called into being to worship God and serve man. The eager, vocal lay response to the critics and a growing theologi-

cal concern *outside* the church are severe judgments on educated parish clergy who, throughout this century, tempered
their competent biblical training and substantial theological
insights to accommodate anti-intellectuals, moralists, and senti-
mentalists in the parishes they served. As honest students of
Scripture know, biblical religion testifies to the God who walks
into the Dachaus of this world and liberates their captives, who
inhabits racial ghettoes and inspirits hopeless inmates, who insists on justice for all people, who associates willingly with the
ignorant and willful who make their bed in any existential
hell. The institutional church, liberal and fundamentalist alike,
had domesticated that God! The "gad-fly" critics let fresh air
into the church and "shook up" the old guard. Probing critics
—Barth, the Niebuhrs, Temple, Tillich, Bonhoeffer, Bultmann
—exposed the church's lack of candor on biblical and theological issues, challenged its deep-seated anti-intellectualism,
and criticized its disengagement from the world.

But these critics did not renew the church. They prepared
the way for renewal. The work of the critics can be likened to
condemnation proceedings, property acquisition, and demoli-
tion of buildings in the complex process of urban renewal.
Getting title to and clearing the land is essential to urban
renewal. But it is *not* renewal.

The church critics called the church to reassess cultural
Christianity and orient radically to biblical Christianity. They
distinguished between religiosity and Christian piety. They
prodded churchmen to determine where traditional language,
ancient liturgies, and historic dogmas are bridges and where
they are barriers between the church and the world. They
reminded the church population that Christianity exists in
God's world. All this was *preparation* for renewal; it was not
renewal. The church experiences new life only when the Word

of God—freed from a Book, liberated from the mists of value judgments, and clothed in meaningful language—confronts persons in their freedom through persons who, exercising their freedom affirmatively, bear witness to God's truth in deed and word.[8] Your question on the relationship between worship and witness gets at the heart of ongoing renewal.

The issue is worship *and* witness. Christian worship "is not a rule of safety." [9] Neither is it a liturgical exercise or a human performance. It is, in fact, the ground on which God confronts man in judgment and grace. Each person responsive to God in worship is empowered to be, like his Lord, the man for others in deed *and* word. If worship does not constrain the worshiper to do God's work in the world, it is not Christian worship. "Why call ye me Lord, Lord, and do not my commandments?" That abrasive question was not invented by this generation of parish critics!

Whoever worships the God of Abraham, Jacob, and Moses, the God of the prophets, the Father of Jesus Christ, grows compassionately aware of the world and gets more involved with persons in messy human situations than those who worship money, sex, family, status, corporation, or nation. Luther reveled in the companionship of his Katie and their boisterous children, insisted on worldly Christianity, and enjoyed controversy with his beer. Wesley and his lay preachers got into the seamy corners of poverty-ridden London in the eighteenth century. Pope John XXIII dialogued with Communists, admired Luther, called the Jews brothers, and blessed a circus. Martin Luther King scaled prophetic heights in a Birmingham jail. Those men were more worldly than those in our day whose claim to "worldliness" rests on reading *Playboy* magazine, *The Love Machine, The Exhibitionist,* and *Couples;* separating sex from love *and* marriage; seeking power for personal advantage; and pursuing pleasure without purpose.

When God speaks to a man in worship, that man speaks and acts for God—in the world. Where else, except in the world, can that witness be made? Jesus retired to Gethsemane; he returned to face Judas, Pilate, Herod—and Calvary. That is as worldly as any man can be! Whoever hears and responds affirmatively to the demands and promises of Christ (true worship) is motivated to evangelize, share liberally, view nuclear weapons with awe, accept the burden of demeaned peoples, be concerned about situational poverty, and so on. Christ —worshiped in an imposing cathedral, a gleaming new church in the round, or an austere meeting house—bids the worshiper to follow him into the world and on to Calvary. The Christ-followers differ in age, background, talent, cultural maturity, and quality of allegiance, but they are alike in this: each brings his Christian insights and concern to bear in and on the world Christ loved and died to save.

Authentic worship of God-in-Christ not only offers the way to creative service in the world and a sense of personal meaningfulness; it also provides the discipline in grace to be *scientific* (objective). This is so because the worship of the Christian God—immanent *and* transcendent—saves the worshiper from accepting *any* particular theory, defined mythology, or fixed dogma as absolute and forever binding. Christian worship provides the context and motivation for inquiry and experimentation. Revelation is not a *thing* to be possessed but the continuing activity of God to be experienced and shared— *here and now.*[10]

The current confusion over worship and witness is as old as Christianity itself. It roots in the centuries-old controversy over *faith and works* which claimed center stage as early as the fourth Christian century when Augustine and Pelagius confronted each other over grace, human freedom, and humane deeds. Luther added a chapter to it. We are writing another. Churchmen will agree that faith without good works is useless. They are not agreed, however, that it is gospel faith which not only produces good works, but works *acceptable to God.* In their concern to *act,* they have minimized (often unwittingly) the need for that Faith which opens man to reconciliation with God through Christ who, accepting man as a forgiven rebel, *empowers* him to love God and neighbor as himself. Paul called this man "justified," "the new man in Christ." Luther presented him as the *"alter Christus."* Bonhoeffer called him "the man for others." Some call him the authentic human. Witness to and service for Christ in the world *demonstrate* the believer's justification, newness, other-person-centeredness, true humanity. But it is Christ who makes man new; good works do not remake man.

No one is saved because he goes to church, prays, tithes, and reads Scripture. Neither is he saved because he works for fair housing, equal educational opportunities, and open employment. This is the new works righteousness in church circles. No human activity, *however useful,* can be substituted for God's deed in Christ. His deed is the only ground for man's justification. But in pressing this argument that authentic Christian worship motivates the worshiper to render specific service to man in a concrete situation, I am not suggesting that a non-Christian's service to his fellowmen is unacceptable to God or meaningless to humanity. Jesus demolished *that* kind of spiritual pride when he warned his disciples against trying to limit God's ways to *their* experience of his deeds.

William Temple declared that he learned to love God through learning to love his fellowmen. What I am pointing out is that (a) man cannot substitute any human deed for God's deed in Christ, and (b) the worship of the Christian God in spirit and truth challenges, motivates, and enables the worshiper to serve humanity (self and others) for Christ's sake. Biblical Christianity rests on Christ's saving work. It is personal *and* social, existential *and* historical, individual *and* corporate. It calls for and inspires worship *and* witness.[11]

But your question not only revives the faith and works issue; it also prompts other crucial questions. How has God acted in the past? What is the significance of history? How do the words of men recorded in the Scriptures testify to the Word of God? What is the dynamic relationship between Scripture and church tradition? (The Roman Catholics are wrestling magnificently with that question.) What is the relationship between God's revelation in history and his revelation in personal experience? In brief, what authority resides in the Bible, tradition, personal experience? Is there a final seat of authority? New life is aborted where individuals and churches shy away from these crucial questions.

The bibliography I'm compiling includes books that helped me with questions of this sort. My priest, Dr. Conrad, brought some of them to my attention. I discovered others for myself. Dialogue with your clergy, but read critically and think for yourself. If the church is to go forward with banners flying, its alert laity must learn to (a) discern the Word of God in the words of men (in Scripture and in contemporary history); (b) think theologically; and (c) reflect God's justice and love through their daily *words* and *deeds*. A subjective faith, however earnest, results in a warped or sterile witness.

Biblical faith is an objective-subjective affair that involves the whole man.

Theologically,

Jim

XVIII

Chicago
15 October, 1969

Dear Prof,

I get what you're driving at. Dr. Jameson agrees with you. But the style of worship and witness in your church is different from the style in mine. And the styles of both churches differ from the style of the free churches. An exchange of views will enlighten both of us. No single tradition in the Faith has more than a segment of truth. Each tradition needs to dialogue and work with the others. As a one-time biblical literalist, I think our catholic-confessional churches have as much to learn from the free churches and sects as those Christian communities have to learn from us.[12] Each tradition has strengths; each has weaknesses. Your church's defensiveness on the episcopacy strikes me as a case in point. My church's reluctance to get involved in the world is another.

Perhaps we can meet in New York. Dr. Jameson, to whom I've confessed all, wants to meet you, the pseudo-architect of his destruction. I've invited him to accompany me to New York next month. Can you and your minister meet us at the Four Seasons for dinner at eight o'clock, Tuesday evening, November 5? You and Jameson will relate famously. I look forward to meeting Dr. Conrad. If he got through to you, he must be an authentic human being.

Our associate ministers have persuaded me to teach a class of high school seniors. The one who is strong for social action, five years younger than I, suggested that I study for a Ph.D. in government at the University of Chicago and enter college teaching! Recalling that Allan Nevins and George Kennan moved from journalism and diplomacy to teaching, writing, and research—and evaluating my fresh interest in ideas and language *and* my current economic affluence—I talked the matter over with Joan. She was surprised, cautious, skeptical, open. I visited the University here and talked with four professors I've come to know in community work. But I decided that, while a teaching career appeals to me intellectually, it would be too confining for my temperament. Instinctively, I made the right decision at graduation—business. Frankly, I would be distressed if Ted, Jr., entered teaching or the ministry. Both professions would be too confining for him, too. He is destined to run a major corporation in A.D. 2002!

Let's have that bibliography. After all, a busy physician named Luke found time to write two Christian treatises for his friend, Theophilus. Who knows—you may wind up in the New Testament! Luther, I learned recently, declared that the canon isn't closed. The implications of that are astounding!

Joan sends her love to you both. She wants Anne to know that she is trying to temper my disregard for your clock!

Cordially,

Ted

XIX

New Canaan
28 October, 1969

Dear Ted,

Your candor is refreshing. Your enthusiasm is contagious. Your spirit is invigorating. Those qualities will get you into hot water with your fellow members. But you are a born controversialist, so enjoy yourself.

Joan is right. You strain a demanding schedule. Along with undergraduate and graduate teaching, research on another book, and service on our parish vestry, I have accepted an appointment to a national church committee to evaluate theological education in our Episcopal Church. I'm not too busy, however, to correspond with a maturing churchman like you —and it's good discipline for me.

The bibliography is enclosed on a separate page.[13] I've starred the books you should begin with. Read for thrust, not detail.

Because you understand the importance of primary documents, you will dig into the Gospels and Epistles daily. But don't limit your study to the New Testament; the Old Testament is essential for solid theological thinking and vigorous witness in the world. Concentrate on the major Prophets, Genesis, Deuteronomy, and the Psalms. Since you enjoy language, read *aloud* from the King James translation of the Gospels and the Prophets. *Listen* as you read. But use the RSV for your studies. You will also profit from reading Augustine's *The City of God;* Luther's *Liberty of the Christian Man,* and Bonhoeffer's *Prison Letters.* Review Locke, Hobbes, Rousseau, Nietzsche, Marx, and Keynes—guided by selected readings from your university days. Re-examine the *Federalist Papers*. Study Lincoln's Second Inaugural Address as a *theological* document.

Subscribe to *Christianity and Crisis* (intellectual), *The Christian Century* (liberal), *Christianity Today* (conservative), and *Commonweal* (liberal Roman Catholic). Read all four regularly.

Academically,

"Prof"

P.S. On the bibliography: concentrate on H. Richard Niebuhr, Tillich, Bultmann, and Ebeling.

XX

Chicago
30 November, 1969

Dear Prof,

Thanks for the bibliography. I should have written sooner, but I was troubleshooting in Europe twice in the last month. And I've been reading avidly.

I subscribed to the magazines you recommended. They're excellent. *Commonweal* fascinates me; I'm amazed at the intellectual stirring in Catholic circles. Incidentally, *Commonweal* speaks often to our Presbyterian "situation." The Christian Church is indeed sociological—and human! *Christianity and Crisis* is my favorite. I've gotten several plane-mates to read an article or two. People *are* interested in ethical and doctrinal matters. All the religious books on your bibliography are in our parish library, but we had few of the secular studies.

With Jameson's grateful approval, I placed Commager, Barzun, Hofstadter, Kohn, Lasch, Ward, Faulkner, Camus, Baldwin, Updike, and Greene on the shelves. At the last Session meeting I asked for ten minutes to present the thesis of Hofstadter's sobering *Anti-Intellectualism in American Life*. Five colleagues promised to read the book!

Evidently, you view the church as a Christianizing community, a culturizing agency, and a brigade for social action. That's medieval and avant garde at the same time, isn't it? But I understand what you're driving at: conservation and innovation, tradition and mission go hand in hand. Teaching high school seniors in our church school has given me a new perspective on youth today. One of Jameson's associates—the traditionalist—encouraged me to read Kenneth Keniston's *Young Radicals*,[14] a study of youth who are actively crusading against war, poverty, racial discrimination, pretense, and so on. I jotted down several quotes. One young radical, noting approvingly that "my old man is very straight with the kids," testified firmly to a creative interaction between tradition and mission: "The values I got from my family, the ones that I've kept, are good. I've pared them and peeled them to fit my own style, but there is a good continuity here. I mean it's a new generation, but there's a lot from the old generation that can't be minimized. Otherwise, I might have flipped out or something like that, or just turned myself off altogether." [15]

Another young radical told his peer group that "my basic rhetoric is a very theological one." Insisting that *that* "rhetoric" turns people off today, he employed it nonetheless: "Maybe if I were born three or four hundred years earlier, I'd be a preacher. I'd say that people should reform, that they should stop being sinners, that they should realize that the world has to be built on different foundations—'Tis the final conflict,'

'Let each man take his place.' (Laughs) . . . My initial thing is
to get up and preach to people and expect them to follow me.
That's where my impulse is, to speak out to the world." [16]

These are not the woebegone, purposeless youth of the 1950's
who, lacking direction, took the tragic James Dean as their
hero. These youth, challenged by John F. Kennedy to become
splendid Americans, sought to be purposeful. During the early
sixties they produced a vigorous outpouring of youthful self-
definition. "Then Kennedy's murder, confirming for these
young people their worst suspicions about the absurdity and
evil of contemporary American society, accelerated their
movement toward a drastic rejection of the existing order—
and, with it, the older generation." [17] The stage was set for
open conflict. The mounting tension between the generations
burst over America like a Fourth of July fireworks display at
an 1890 community gathering: alienation—"you can't trust
anyone over thirty"; demonstrations for civil rights and
against the war in Vietnam; draft-card burnings; urban and
campus riots; the cult of the "hippies" (free love, psychedelic
drugs, and life as "happening"). Both the revolutionaries and
the social dropouts, suspicious of every power structure, attacked our "values." Although the revolutionaries and social
dropouts are a minority among our youth, many of their questions are eloquent and many of their critiques are relevant.
It was crusading youth, 1966-68, who pressed for a critical
re-examination of patriotism, influenced a "consensus" President's decision to step down, and moved the academic community off dead center! Churchmen, educators, and politicians
must dialogue creatively with them. Working together, both
generations must forge more humane values and goals. I'm
trying! I want a church *and* a social-political community where
the middle-aged and the youth, the white and the black, the

affluent and the poverty-ridden, the educated and the un-educated—worship God and speak and do the truth in love to and for one another.

Cordially,

Ted

XXI

Nassau
20 December, 1969

Dear Ted,

You have written perceptively on the dynamic relation between tradition and mission, and on the real and potential social-political impact of our youth. Working daily with young people, I agree substantially with your judgments. I shared your letter with Dr. Conrad, who plans to incorporate it in a future sermon. I also placed the Keniston book in our parish library. Our Parish Education Committee is recommending it to the church school teachers. Some young people are closer to the living traditions of our Judeo-Christian heritage than they realize. But too many still opt, like their fathers, for "the fleshpots of Egypt." They seek safety, security, and serenity.

Your letter sent me to my files for a quotation from John Dos Passos: "In time of change and danger when there is quicksand of fear under men's reasoning, a sense of continuity with generations gone before can stretch like a life-line across the scary present." [18] Conservation and innovation, tradition and mission—constantly in tension—structure the healthy society and the dynamic institution. Jesus did not abrogate the past; he fulfilled its promises beyond expecta-

93

tion. He did not destroy the Law; he enlarged its compass immeasurably. He brought a New Age into history. But Moses, the Prophets, and John the Baptist had prepared the way. Everyone has a "past"—even Jesus (the lineage of David; *and,* "In the beginning . . . the Word was with God")!

The future of our nation is impenetrable. Its present is unpredictable. But its past provides an exciting present and suggests a creative future! Three hundred and fifty action-packed years since the settlement of Jamestown provide a firm preparation for the severe testing of our democratic society today. But those traditions of freedom, individual liberty, and justice are older than three centuries. From this present era, they reach back through Lincoln and Jefferson, Locke and Montesquieu, Luther and Calvin, to the philosophers of Greece and the prophets of Judea. Those traditions are woven into the fabric of our American life. Our heritage suggests that we are equipped to show young people and oppressed citizens in this nation, and in all nations, "that the revolutionary ideals which had begun so valiantly in 1776 would not rest until the rights of man had been established everywhere in the world." [19] It is our moral responsibility to be true to *that* heritage!

Anne joins me in wishing Joan and you and the children a blessed Christmas and continued growth as persons in the New Year.

Cordially,

Jim

XXII

Chicago
8 February, 1970

Dear Prof,

The reading course is underway. Hofstadter, Commager, Ward, and H. Richard Niebuhr are provocative, comprehensible, enlightening. Tillich, Bultmann, and Ebeling are simply too steep for me. I'm terribly confused over the relationship between the Word of God and the words of men. At the same time, I *am* challenged by the relationship between meaning and language; history and present experience.

I've been discussing these complex problems with Dr. Jameson. If I understand him, he is saying that *exegesis* has to do with discovering what was in the mind of the biblical writer when *he* wrote and with the historical situation *he* was addressing; and *interpretation* is what a particular biblical truth means to us now. Jameson told me to rely on competent commentators for exegesis, study the text carefully and prayerfully, and, when it speaks to me, put its meaning into relevant language and effective deeds. He says that hermeneutics is simply the methodology of getting from exegesis to interpretation. Simple! It's so damn complex I'm ready to quit. Yet, I think I do get the drift of it.

Ebeling argues that the basic problem has to do with how an event nineteen hundred years ago is to be understood as affecting life today. Bultmann argues that all Scripture must be demythologized; he is convinced that modern man won't listen to the church talk about God as long as it uses the language of "myth." But there is a thin line between mythological and logical descriptions of reality. For example, I accept the "stories" of the Creation and the Fall as "myth," but I don't agree that those stories are to be understood only in terms of *my* human experience. There is larger truth in them than that. They point to a massive downward turn in human nature itself which only God's deed in Christ can reverse. I certainly agree with Bultmann that anyone who talks seriously about God must also talk about man. But I cringe when Bultmann suggests that the incarnation and atonement have meaning only in my discovering *my* authentic personhood in them. This denigration of history is irrational.

As I see it, Bultmann blurs the objective nature of God's deed in Christ (that Event outside man's prior experience) by separating Christ and his gospel from history. That's like saying that Lincoln's Second Inaugural Address was "for real" because *I* feel it was real. Actually, it was real because (a) it was conceived and delivered by a particular man in a particular place in a particular moment of history; (b) it enunciated "truths" that spoke to many of his contemporaries; and (c) it speaks to some people *now*. Christ is relevant to man, Bultmann argues, because Christ rings true for *him!* That's too subjective. I think Ebeling gets closer to reality when he argues that "the truth that makes man true lies outside himself —that is his basic situation." [20] Paul Tillich, focusing on *Being,* also speaks to me, because I *do* face up to that moment when *I* will cease to *be.* Interestingly, I have realized lately that facing that possibility each time I flew a bombing mission years ago actually strengthened my "fundamentalist" faith in God! Ebeling, Bultmann, and Tillich appeal to me because they face honestly some of the complex questions on reality, meaning, and language—and insist that the church do the same.

This makes fascinating study, but I haven't time for it

nor am I equipped to pursue it. No wonder devout American church members venerate the Bible as an object of faith rather than dig into it as an inspired human record of God's deeds in history—or ignore it altogether. It's easier that way. No wonder *concerned* churchmen go all out for social action. Even discussions on social issues let them "feel" involved! You bit off more than I can chew when you placed Bultmann, Tillich, and Ebeling in the bibliography. You are experienced in reading at that level; I'm not. Furthermore, I get the impression that biblical scholars and professional theologians write for each other. Their work has an "ingroup" flavor that irritates me. Why can't they write like Hofstadter, Schlesinger, and Galbraith, and like Robinson, Fletcher, and Cox? That style of writing is understandable and interesting!

Vexedly yours,

Ted

XXIII

New Canaan
7 March, 1970

Dear Ted,

Ebeling, Bultmann, and Tillich are not too much for you. Your substantial beginning proves that. Formally educated and intellectually alert laymen can and must read at that level so that they can speak relevantly to probing, questing people outside Christianity. Admittedly, there are many laymen who cannot read this kind of theological literature. Neither can they read Freud, Barzun, or Gardner. They are not inclined or equipped in this age of "instant knowledge" to decipher "trapped ideas" on a printed page; they are not able or willing to wrestle with language and meaning. These persons in the church (and outside) must be attracted and persuaded by biblical preaching and teaching, relevant dialogical encounters, bold deeds of Christian service—*and* by sensate media—liturgy, music, art, drama, movies, and TV.

McLuhan highlights this judgment when he reminds us that writing the words "American flag" across a piece of cloth would deprive the "rich visual mosaic of the Stars and Stripes . . . of most of its qualities of corporate image and of experience." [21] Precisely! Printed words are not the only media for communicating God's Word. Liturgical forms, Christian symbols, pageantry, art, drama, and TV are also media that can carry the Christian message to people in this generation. The issue is not either/or; it is both/and.

But the printed word is not passé. After all, McLuhan wrote a book to disseminate *his* sweeping conclusions! The American people expended 2 1/3 billion dollars for books in 1968. Intellectually alert laymen must study at the verbal level if the local congregation is to keep pace with today's knowledge explosion. In the last third of this explosive (knowledge) century, it is crucial that educated people get a religious education comparable to their general education if they are to become genuinely human and the church is to speak persuasively. A century and a quarter ago, Wendell Phillips spoke to *our* generation of educated people when he argued: "College-bred men should be agitators to tear a question open and riddle it with light and to educate the moral sense of the masses."

Address yourself to these questions. What is the relationship between the words of men and the Word of God? What is the unity in the hodgepodge of books called the Bible? Is it Christ?[22] Brood over language, meaning, reality. That is precisely what you do in making a meaningful marriage and in motivating your sales force to sell farm machinery! Employ the *same* critical faculties to forge your faith, formulate your theology, and make your witness.

Keep wrestling with the *message* in the biblical records. If you expose yourself to that message, it will redirect your present expectations, reshape your existential questions, and introduce you to new values. Your world view differs radically from that of the biblical writers, but they can challenge, correct, and enlarge your cultural conception of reality. An alert high school freshman knows more about the physical universe and the biophysical-psychological structure of man than the biblical writers (pre-Copernicus, pre-Harvey, and pre-Freud). But those ancients knew more, being open to revelation, about the nature of God and the existential needs of man than you or I or Freud or the freshman! Stay with it, Ted. Revelation is not a religious *thing* to be possessed; it is an ongoing activity of God to be experienced, examined, acted on.

Please drop the "Prof" bit. I do have a Christian name.

Fraternally,

Jim

XXIV

Chicago
22 March, 1970

Dear Jim,

Your answer on Bultmann, *et al.,* is disconcerting because I recognize its pertinence. Unless educated laymen manage an intellectual understanding of the Scriptures' witness to God, fashion a conceptual-existential rationale for the church's involvement in contemporary society, encourage their clergy to speak for God, and challenge other laymen to follow Christ *into the world,* the church will become increasingly irrelevant in our technological society. An enlightened pew, posing probing questions and seeking ways to humanize society, could lift the level of preaching and lay witness in half a decade. These stabbing lines from John Updike's *The Same Door*—an armchair critique of contemporary preaching—are an indictment of intellectuals who find it easier to be critical of the church than to get involved with persons in and through its fellowship for Christ's sake. "Sunday morning: waking, he . . . lacked the will to get up, to unfurl the great sleepy length beneath the covers and to be disillusioned in the ministry by some servile, peace-of-mind-peddling preacher. If it wasn't peace of mind, it was the integrated individual, and if it wasn't the integrated individual, it was the power hidden within each one of us. Never a stern old commodity like sin or remorse, never an open-faced superstition. So he decided, without pretending that it was the preferable course as well as the easier, to stay home and read Saint Paul." [23]

That "Dear Jim" salutation jars me. I knew you wanted it used, yet I hesitated. A psychiatrist might suggest that I

100

wanted to keep a student-teacher relationship so I could hold you partially responsible for the outcome of my life. However, I think it's as simple as this: I was reared to respect my elders. You made a durable impression on me as "Prof." To me, you are a distinguished "elder." Nonetheless, you want me to recognize that our relationship is changing; and, of course, it is. O.K., Jim, I can walk now. Someday I shall run. I'm indebted to you.

Cordially,

Ted

XXV

Mid-Atlantic, Pan Am Jet
25 June, 1970

Dear Jim,

Three months without a letter from the executive-theologian. But I haven't been drifting; I've been doing my homework. I've read extensively and intensively, pondered and meditated. I've conversed daily with all sorts of people— clergy, church members, unchurched colleagues at work, and total strangers. My frequent air trips used to bore me; now they provide time for study and serious conversation. I pack more books than shirts for business trips these days. It's amazing how much serious reading one can do and how much meaningful conversation one can manage if he decides to.

Before I provide a résumé of my current thinking on the Word of God in the words of men, let me say I have come to appreciate the significance of the 1967 Confession of

Faith that my United Presbyterian Church hammered out in blood, sweat, and tears. As I understand the broad picture, the rising struggle over fundamentalism in my church surfaced in the Briggs controversy at Union Theological Seminary in the 1890's when that institution freed itself from a Presbyterian Church that was less than candid about the results of biblical scholarship. The unresolved struggle which underlay that widening schism became embarrassingly evident in the Machen controversy at Princeton Seminary four decades ago.[24] But the essential controversy smoldered until the General Assembly approved the Confession of 1967. This courageous document squares us at last with modern biblical scholarship and brings us face to face with man-in-society during the last third of the twentieth century.

I know there's still heat in the theological kitchen of our merged Presbyterian Church. That's wholesome. The clean-cut statements on the Word of God expose the anti-intellectuals, confront the paper popes, and stand firmly against the absolute demythologizers. The call to involvement in society is equally significant. In particular, the section that declares that the Christian honors God's will above the aims of his national state spells out that which is inherent in any believer's honest acceptance of Christ: one can't serve two masters honorably. The furor stirred by that part of the document reveals the biblical illiteracy, theological naïveté, and cultural religiosity in our church. Of course, the "Bishop Pike Affair" and similar ecclesiastical fumblings convince me that you Episcopalians sweep your problems under the rug![25] I suppose all denominations try to keep the lid on explosive situations. Openness and candor are not Protestantism's long suit. One wing of Catholicism outruns us these days. At any rate, my United Presbyterian Church had the temerity to bring its confession of faith into line with biblical scholarship and the courage to cast it in contemporary language. I'm proud to be a member of a church like that.

These are the maturing judgments that presently guide me in interpreting the Bible and making my "witness." (1) The Reformation view of the priesthood of believers must be rescued from its violent distortion in the contemporary church: an "everyman-his-own-boss" doctrine. Laymen must learn that they are members of the Body of Christ and that he is the Head. Authority resides in Christ. Consequently, Scripture, tradition, and local parish practices must be interpreted in the light of Christ's person, work, and teachings. Presently, that is not the procedure.

(2) Scripture is the inspired human record (employing the words of men) of God's progressive intervention in the course of human history. His self-revelation is communicated through myth, legend, drama, historical events, historical persons (Moses, Isaiah, Jeremiah), and finally in the historical Jesus (the Gospels). Firsthand evidence on the Resurrection Christ and his new community is recorded in Acts and the Epistles. The oral tradition, preserved in the New Testament, cannot be completely demythologized without losing the flesh and blood Jesus. There is an irreducible minimum; he was born in the days of Caesar Augustus and ministered, suffered, was crucified and resurrected during the governorship of Pontius Pilate. That is the testimony of hardheaded men in *their* portraits and interpretations of a particular Person who lived in a particular time in a particular place. The Christian Faith roots in history; the gospel is inseparable from human events. Simon Peter was plainspoken on that: "We have not followed cunningly devised fables." Jameson insists that the methodology of the demythologizers and the symbolists undercuts the

historical foundations of the Christian Faith. He calls them the new subjectivists. He says they denigrate history and "vaporize" God. I agree. But Jameson does not appreciate fully the significant contributions that Bultmann and Tillich made by attacking anti-intellectualism in the church. Both men certainly helped me to understand the Living Word—Christ. Fact and value, history and faith, are integral pieces in Christian revelation and experience. Confessional churches concentrate on the former; evangelical churches focus on the latter. But either apart from the other distorts the good news and subverts one's effective witness to it.

(3) To understand what God said and did in "biblical history" is to gain a perspective on what he is saying and doing now—and vice-versa. Unless one is exposed to the Scripture's witness to God's activity in the past, he is not likely to be aware of God's activity in the present, nor is he likely to find objective ground for hope in the future. Study, teaching, and preaching that is truly biblical is never simply historical. When it is authentically biblical—the living God confronting persons through persons in their contemporary situation—it is existential. The church must be concerned with God's saving *deed*, completed once and for all, and it must be concerned equally with God's saving activity *now* on the basis of that unique act. This—the source of renewal in the church—is personal and social. God desires the sinner's justification through faith in Christ. Equally, he wants "justified" men to work for social justice (civil righteousness) so that all people have an open opportunity to become genuinely human.

(4) To act on God's demands and promises, to doubt and question, to trust and obey, to know and do and hope—this *is* Christian faith. It is objective-subjective. Plato agrees with

Christ on this: one does not truly "know" something until he acts on it. Jesus urged men to "test the doctrine."

Finally, it seems to me that contemporary theology has neglected God in nature. The church, inquiring into "God in history" and "God in personal experience," lags badly in probing into "God in nature" (conservation of natural resources, pollution control, prayer in the light of the new physics, and so on). The ecology of our planet demands that we get more familiar with the balance of nature before we keep fooling with forces that may be out of control even now. We may be working on our own Tower of Babel. The times are hospitable for such inquiry. The new sciences provide a fresh intellectual climate for it; the failure of atheistic rationalism and benign humanism to improve the lot of all people suggests it; the growing openness between some churchmen and some agnostic intellectuals promises a fruitful encounter. One of my colleagues, a vice-president in charge of engineering and a devout Roman Catholic, introduced me to Pierre Teilhard de Chardin. That abused priest's magnificent synthesis of science and Christian faith is a pioneering venture that suggests some bridges between the disciplines of theology and science. My colleague has been a vocal Christian since he discovered that Chardin interpreted creation in evolutionary terms and the real presence (Lord's Supper) as a form of energy. My friend argues cogently that prayer, the Incarnation, and the Trinity are more intelligible in the light of the new sciences of physics and psychology than in terms of a mechanical science and a static moral philosophy. We need more theological writing like Chardin's.

Well, that's my term paper on the Bible, the Word of God, the church, and theology. The research, reading, study, and conversations have been enriching and maturing. I intend to keep at it. I'm becoming intensely concerned about my place in political and economic affairs as a Christian *citizen*. I am convinced that God-in-Christ has turned the world over to man.

Gratefully,

Theodore Tillich Connors

XXVI

Bar Harbor, Maine
10 July, 1970

Dear Ted,

You are developing a solid, relevant theology. Splendid! Encourage others to work at it, too. Until the local church —led and taught by persons able to interpret Scripture with Christ as guide—manages some intellectually sophisticated "God-talk," cultural Christianity and sentimental religiosity will obscure the God of the Bible. Until the American parish discerns and accepts God's authority in Christ—and an objective view of Scripture and a critical stance on tradition is necessary for that—segments in each parish, entire congregations, and denominational splinter groups will ride off, like Leacock's horseman, in all directions at the same time.

Ted, you read like a man starved for ideas—as you did years ago at the University. You pursue truth objectively and subjectively. You are responsibly involved in getting better housing and fair employment practices in your city. In my judgment, your present vocation doesn't tap the full range of your splendid talents. I'm not underestimating your place in the business community or belittling that community. Populated with able minds, imaginative spirits, and resilient people, the business community has provided real talent to our government: Harriman, Rockefeller, Dillon, Scranton, Romney, McNamara, Percy, and others. That is precisely the point I want to make. You belong in politics!

It's not too late for you to enter the political arena. The vocation of politics is open to you and other mature, successful intellectual activists—at any age. John Lindsay is a young man; Averill Harriman is almost eighty. Get involved in local politics; see where it leads. You may discover that it is *your* true vocation.

Several years ago, the Rhodesian political detainee, Ndabaningi Sithole, observed that most of the important political leaders in Africa today had attended mission schools. He declared that "the Bible is now doing what we could not do with our spears." [26] He also said that the Christian Church had fashioned a Christian consciousness that, transcending old barriers of race and color, now gives "creative purpose and direction to African national consciousness." [27] That has been true in American political experience, too. Unfortunately, neither generation is alert to God's activity in history.

For those who lack a sense of history, America's legal separation of political and religious institutions has obscured the *influence* of each on the other in the development of our national state *and* our churches. The Founding Fathers were not anti-religion; they were anti-establishment.[28] Deists like Jefferson and Franklin and orthodox Christians like Adams (Congregational), Madison (Episcopal), Washington (Episcopal), and Carroll (Roman Catholic) were aware that a man's faith (or lack of it) influences his social and political expectations, thoughts, and deeds. On the Continent, an eighteenth-century deist, Middleton, argued that, while the Christian faith was unacceptable to intellectuals, "a good citizen will support Christianity and the Christian Church as a bulwark of social order, providing admirable deterrents to the barbarism latent in mankind." I'm not suggesting that one should embrace Christianity because, domesticated, it guarantees the social *status quo*. Actually, serious Christians criticize and disturb unjust social orders—Alan Paton in South Africa and Father Groppi in Milwaukee demonstrate that! What I'm pointing out is that earnest Christians, aware that God has turned the world over to them in Christ, work diligently to fashion a social and political society that allows and encourages *all* its citizens to become truly human.

During the nineteenth century, Christian traditionalists deliberately joined rationalists and humane secularists to build a stable political society in America. Theology went begging in the nineteenth century because this activistic alliance between religion and politics was noncritical, but the alliance *was* fostered in those decades and was influential.

The post-Revolutionary separation of church and state in America—a separation of the *institutions* of the religious community and the political society—was a stroke of genius. But to suppose, as so many Americans now do in violation of the mind of the Founding Fathers, that the two communities are mutually exclusive, is ahistorical and anti-intellectual. Our citizenry must be challenged on that. The view is also unbiblical. Churchmen must be challenged on *that*. Amos collided with the political power structure of his day because he attacked the economic injustices in his society. Pharaoh pursued the fleeing Israelites, not to provide a chase scene for a Cecil B. DeMille movie, but because Moses had shattered the base of Egypt's socioeconomic structure—slavery. Jesus was charged formally with threatening the political stability of the Roman Empire. Paul was forced to flee Ephesus because his preaching threatened the economic security of the local silversmiths who manufactured replicas of the goddess Diana. The early Christians, accepting God as sovereign, undercut the Emperor's prestige and power, thereby weakening the political structure of the Roman Empire. Gibbon was right in *that* historical judgment. Informed citizens in and out of the church recognize that Christianity has influenced the American experiment—and still does.

Politics in a free society provides an effective medium for bringing one's Christian insights to bear on concrete situations in order to create a more humane society for the sake of the kingdom of God. In my judgment politics is the most powerful single instrument for social change at the present time; government is an instrumentality through which God works. Man can cooperate. Indeed, he must. Recently, Harvey Wheeler underscored that obligation: "In unconsciously creating a unitary industrial order, man has made his survival depend upon his ability to follow it by a consciously created political order." [29] The American Church—fragmented by multiple, diverse traditions—is not structured institutionally to provide social cohesion, nor is it appointed to offer national direction. Its real impact on society must come from individuals and "remnant groups" who address particular persons, specific issues, and concrete situations. Presently in America, politics is the most effective medium for confrontation, dialogue, and action directed toward social change.

You, Ted, possess the intellect, liberal education, experience, personal contacts, and economic resources to serve effectively in the political arena. Do it. Years ago—you were scarcely seventeen—you exaggerated your age and joined the Air Force. You risked life and limb to preserve free political societies and give them a fresh chance to establish a stable world community. Competent, compassionate, imaginative politicians are essential if that chance is to be realized in this revolutionary century. Knowing you as a person, I am convinced that politics is *your* true vocation. Harvey Cox hit the nail on the head when he wrote: 'To say that speaking of God must be political means that it must engage people at particular points, not just 'in general.' . . . It must be a word . . . which builds peace in a nuclear world, which contributes to justice in an age stalked by hunger, which hastens the day of freedom in a society stifled by segregation." [30]

Proddingly,

Jim

XXVII

Chicago
26 July, 1970

Dear Jim,

You insist that I cease calling you "Prof" and then proceed to lecture me on American political history as though I were a high school sophomore. Damn it, man, you are arrogant!

I recognize that politics is an essential vocation in a free society. Don't tutor me. I recognize the complex interdependence of our urban-technological society. I appreciate that political decisions affect *all* areas of human existence, including the business community. I applauded Truman when he relieved MacArthur for undercutting national policy. I supported Stevenson when he labored to ease Soviet-American tensions. I applauded Hammarskjold's selfless efforts to make the UN an effective instrument for peace. I approved Kennedy's confrontation of Big Steel, cheered his "Ich bin ein Berliner" speech, and admired his moral decision on civil rights in 1963. Don't lecture me on political and social realities, *Prof.* I'm not a displaced "robber baron" from 1880, a business tycoon from 1910, a Babbitt from 1925, or a contemporary wheeler-dealer. Not for a moment have I ever thought that "the business of America is business." I appreciate Hofstadter's *American Political Tradition,* Galbraith's *Affluent Society,* and critical works of that caliber as much as you do.

The point I'm making is that politics is not *my* cup of tea. I'm even less suited temperamentally for that vocation than for a career in the academic community. Both vocations are crucial in a democracy, but neither appeals to me. I'm a businessman, a company man, an organization man in the best sense of those hackneyed phrases—and I'm proud of it. Why don't *you* enter the political arena if you're so damned sold on politics as a vocation? I have other fish to fry.

Our corporation is facing tougher competition in Europe as well as in the States. Aiming at the corporation presidency, I can't afford to take my nose from the grindstone. Politicking and fence-mending are as important as ability and performance. There is "room at the top" of the mammoth American corporations, but getting there requires more emotional control than achieving any other power position in our society except the American presidency. You simply don't understand the severe intellectual and emotional demands on top business executives in these days of domestic and international competition and sociopolitical change. Get off my back!

111

Meanwhile, I'm getting into rough waters in my congregation. The Affable Enemy is rocking my boat. Several fellow board members resent my energetic involvement in parish life; others resist my outspoken demands that the church confront persons and power structures in this urban jungle of Chicago. Motivated by a sense of noblesse oblige rather than Christian love, our members are willing to help only those who cannot threaten *their* situation. We also have a regiment of mossbacks who, fearing blacks, poor whites, youth, and liberals, react rather than act. Those first letters you wrote on subversion in the local congregation described our members more accurately than I realized at the time. The local parish is a bastion of the *status quo,* a fortress of anti-intellectualism, a stockpile of prejudices. The unconscious subversives are in control.

Instead of badgering me to enter politics you should encourage me in my labors in this congregation. I'm weary in well-doing. The results are slim, the thanks are thin. I doubt that either of Jameson's young associates will remain in the parish ministry. No wonder so many parish clergy are seeking insulated berths as church administrators and professors, fleeing from congregation to congregation, or leaving the church to make their livelihood in other vocations. The parish is a mess, and the presbyteries (synods, dioceses, conferences) are not structured for flexible, relevant action. Ecclesiastical bureaucrats are equipped to preside, administer, plan; they are not equipped to lead. And the few who are able to lead are frustrated by rigid, obsolete ecclesiastical structures. Radical church renewal *cannot* occur in this generation.

I agree with Harvey Cox, who, combining crisis theology with the ethics of Rauschenbush's social gospel, argues that urbanization and secularization confront the Christian church with exciting challenges and rich opportunities. Unfortunately, church members fear *those* challenges and back away from *those* opportunities. The church—inextricably bound into a white, middle-class affluent society—cannot heal itself. In most congregations the clerical and elected (entrenched) lay leaders *are* the problem. The blind cannot lead the blind. Even where clerical leadership is strong, the results are negligible. Here at Overlook Presbyterian Church our clergy, who face up to the problems of American society, are light years ahead of our members and elected lay leaders. Our clergy are heard but not heeded; they are respected as persons but their prophetic witness is blunted by most of our members. Overlook Church does not proclaim Christ persuasively. Our dignified congregation, proud of its *paid* prophets-in-residence, uses them to insulate itself against serious involvement in society!

I'm sick of this mess. You were right the first time around: the church is *absolute* deadweight on those who seek justice now.

Disgusted and discouraged,

Ted

XXVIII

Bar Harbor, Maine
6 August, 1970

Dear Ted,

Here you are, crying the blues again. This time you're wounded because your fellow members haven't given you the Distinguished Service Medal for your valorous service. Do you need the sweet smell of success to keep at a job? Do you require the Air Force Band to bolster you? My heart bleeds for you, Golden Boy. Certainly it's hard to be a Christian in the local congregation *and* in the church bureaucracies, the colleges and seminaries, business, politics, and the family. It always has been difficult. Every faltering disciple since Simon Peter will testify to that.

I'm often tempted to pursue truth as a research scholar. The professor's life is *not* the cloistered existence you think it is. The academic community needs renewal as urgently as the church requires it. Creative teaching, challenging students to pursue excellence, and motivating them to serve persons are costly goals to realize in *any* institutional setting. Recasting institutional forms that enable persons to confront reality— every administrator's primary responsibility—is as enervating for university presidents, bishops, and congressmen as it is for you and others in local congregations—and it's a *lonelier* life.

Did you expect Overlook Church to be transformed suddenly because you decided to place *your* talents at its service? You were part of the problem long enough to be realistic on that score. At best, you are a catalytic agent of the gospel. Furthermore, results are not *your* primary business. Steadfastness in the Faith is what God expects of you. The Holy Spirit will use your fidelity to the Word as God sees fit.

Stephen was stoned. Paul was crucified. Hus was burned at the stake. Luther was a political refugee. Wesley labored in poverty. Bonhoeffer was hanged. Dibelius was harassed by the Nazis and the Communists. Dr. Jameson has endured his share of hardship like a good soldier of Jesus Christ. But Ted Connors, air ace, honor graduate, skyrocketing executive, custodian of an expanding stock portfolio—brushed by envy and discouraged by smidgins of appreciation—wants to retreat into casual membership and evade his responsibilities as a talented, educated, well-heeled churchman and citizen. You're showing the other face of the Affable Enemy—weariness in well-doing and cowardice in the face of criticism. You are trying to save yourself and the church. It is not your task to do either. You are called to bear witness to Christ. The Holy Spirit breathes new life into persons, creating a new community, the church.

Paul had a promising colleague like you. His name was Demas. But he failed to run a good race. His biography is written in two words: "Demas quit." Don't chicken out— Colonel! Your 8th Air Force did not liberate Europe on its own. *That* event was a costly, massive, *cooperative* venture. In spiritual warfare the stakes are higher, the Enemy is more skillful, the campaigns are longer, the battles are more costly.

Stay and fight!

Regards,

Jim

XXIX

Chicago
9 September, 1970

Dear Jim,

Forget that last letter. The day I wrote it, I wasn't the man I really want to be. Your harsh rebuke was called for. I'll falter often in the years ahead, but I'll not quit as long as I am confronted with the Truth and supported in the community of Faith. This time, you and Jameson provided the help I needed.

A week after I received your letter, and still furious, I phoned Dr. Jameson, made an appointment, and poured out my frustrations. After listening patiently to my laments, Jameson admitted to frequent negative feelings of his own and identified several of them. He assured me that all serious Christians experience seasons when they want to throw in the sponge. Then he selected from his expansive library Reinhold Niebuhr's Gifford Lectures, *The Nature of Man,* and read the opening sentence: "Man has always been his own most vexing problem." [31] Next, he chose Pascal's *Pensées* and read that Christian intellectual's summation of man: "What a chimera then is man, what a novelty, what a monster, what chaos, what a subject of contradiction, what a prodigy! Judge of all things, yet an imbecile earthworm; depository of truth, yet a sewer of uncertainty and error; pride and refuse of the universe." [32] We talked for an hour or so on those suggestive appraisals of human nature.

Most helpful, however, was Jameson's earthy conversation on Jeremiah whom he knows as well as I know the men on my sales force. He told me that Jeremiah is his favorite prophet, because Jeremiah speaks to his (Jameson's) experience. During our conversation, I realized for the first time that Jameson gets angry with God. Indeed, he gets so furious that he accuses God of being a double-dealer! Occasionally, he vents his frustrations on God. The discovery amazed me. Sensing that, Jameson pointed out that if a parent can understand a hostile child and *accept* him in spite of his attacks, God can certainly understand and accept a hostile man. Pouring out my feelings that day, I learned that confession, earthy and honest, is therapeutic and healing.

Finally, Jameson—pointing to Jesus' "Why?" on Calvary, and Paul's "wretched man" confession—reminded me that man must struggle with this dark side of his nature until death sets him free. "Ted," he said, "that's why you and I need a Savior." In our two-hour conversation I discovered what it means to have a confessor, helper, friend, shepherd. The Christian pilgrimage is demanding, but no one needs to walk alone. Perhaps I can help someone over a difficult hurdle someday.

Fraternally,

Ted

XXX

New Canaan
11 September, 1970

Dear Ted,

It's as unchristian to brood over yesterday's failures as it is to boast over last week's successes. Your letter of lament is forgotten. Everyone fails to realize his full humanity in Christ, but failure confessed and *repented* of is failure blotted out. William Temple described repentance as the adoption of God's viewpoint in place of one's own. That's a daily exercise for the Christian.

My dark nights of the soul may be more grim than yours, Ted. Our temperaments are decidedly different. I brood; you complain. Private and corporate confession, set in traditional Christian language, mean incalculably much to me. I'm a natural Episcopalian! You unload through noisy complaints and angry conversations. So long as one goes to God with his frustrations and failures, and renewed, begins afresh, he's on a steady course to realizing his true humanity. Paul Tillich put it simply: a Christian knows he's unacceptable, yet he accepts

God's acceptance of him. That's where authentic personhood begins.

Your counter-challenge that I should enter politics deserves a candid answer. I would like to get in but (a) I can't afford to economically; (b) I'm too pedantic; (c) I lack charisma; (d) I feel that I *am* serving our political society as a professor of government *and* as a consultant to the Federal Department of Urban Affairs, *and* as a member-at-large on our state committee. You may not concur in these judgments, but I have answered your challenge frankly.

On the other hand, *your* political assets are vastly more substantial than mine. (a) You can afford to get involved in politics; (b) your temperament and experience equip you for the rigors of public life; (c) your present vocation does not tap your potential; (d) you possess charisma.

Indefatigably,

Jim

V

A NEW STYLE OF LIVING

It is always difficult to represent the place that power actually holds in the workings of politics and in the processes of history. Some men seem ready to speak as though power did not exist (because in their view it ought not exist); and if others are emphatic about the reality of its presence they are assumed to be in favor of force, merely because they recognize its operation in the world. Others again assert the place of power in history, but do it with an unseemly relish, as though they would not wish the situation to be otherwise. . . . We, for our part, are inclined to believe that the victory of the democracies in two world wars has never been the victory of sheer force, and was only made possible by the collaboration of moral factors. . . .

The world being constituted as it is, even power can perform a good function in society, when it imposes peace and establishes order over a wide region, thereby enabling the work of civilization to proceed and creating a field within which men may grow in reasonableness.[1]

—HERBERT BUTTERFIELD

XXXI

Chicago
26 November, 1970

Dear Jim,

During this year's sporadic correspondence, I've refrained from commenting on two particular experiences in my life. I wanted to evaluate each carefully before discussing them with you.

First, I gained a convert to Christianity—a hardheaded surgeon whom I met a year ago at a cocktail party. A door opened one evening when, in a discussion on the meaning of history, I spoke of divine revelation as God's purposeful intervention in human affairs. A spirited conversation ensued. Several weeks later he invited me to lunch to pursue the conversation. That discussion became a weekly event. An exciting friendship grew between us. Finally, after declining my numerous invitations to attend our church, he came one Sunday. He took to Jameson's preaching, worshiped regularly, questioned relentlessly, enrolled in our New Members' Class, and was baptized. Serious about the Faith, he speaks intelligibly about it and existentially from it with patients, colleagues, and friends.

I've gotten others to join our church, but they were transfers from churches in other communities or other sections of the metropolitan area. My doctor friend is a convert, and in a way, I got two for one! His wife, who had drifted from the church over the years, returned with him.

But this evangelism-in-depth requires hours of dialogue, patience, and *intercessory* prayer. Truth attracts some persons, repels others, and bores many. Human nature is ambivalent, perverse, slothful. Paul could list only a handful of struggling congregations after a lifetime of exhausting labors. I've won only one convert. As far as I can see, I've failed to get through to anyone else. When indifference, evasiveness, cultural disdain, or hostility dishearten me, I examine my style of witness and my person. I also remind myself that Christ won only one of two men on Calvary—and that it was thirty-seven years before he got through to me!

Jameson declares from the pulpit that every man is "free to go to hell." He also declares that every man is free to come home whenever he chooses. Another firm strand in Jameson's preaching is that God judges each Christian on his fidelity to the Living Word rather than on the results achieved. Evangelism is not a program for getting members for the church. It is the personal telling and demonstration of what God has done in Christ. The teller is free to keep silent even as the hearer is free to reject both the good news *and* its bearer. Kierkegaard was right: human freedom *is* dreadful! But human freedom is a dynamic strand in the historical-existential context in which man, deciding for or against Christ, grows into or escapes authentic personhood. It is part of the context in which man accepts or rejects Christ, deciding for or against *whole* life.

Well, I've leaped into politics with both feet! I'm up to my neck in the swirling mess. That's my other bit of news. Presently, I'm serving as publicity chairman for my party's County Committee. Frankly, this cross-section of society startled, jarred, sobered me. Their hopes and fears and strengths and foibles fascinate me. Politics in a free society *is* a viable means to effect social change. I'm hooked, Jim. I'm getting in deeper every day. I'm grateful for your prodding.

One thing more—Ted, Jr., almost sixteen, wants to attend

my University. His academic-athletic-social record indicates that he will qualify for admission. He plans to study law and enter politics. I'm delighted.

Sincerely,
Ted

The correspondence for 1971-76 was unavailable to the editor. But the following letters, written in 1976, will scarcely surprise the alert reader.

XXXII

Chicago
10 November, 1976

Dear Jim,

I'm in the Slough of Despond!

This year's election in our state was as tight as the disputed Hayes-Tilden contest of 1876—and as exhausting! Serving as State Chairman for our party, I've cussed you out time and again for getting me into politics. It's rugged, frustrating, exhausting. Business competition is cleaner. I now understand how "Engine Charlie" Wilson got his foot in his mouth as soon as he joined Eisenhower's Cabinet and how McNamara looked back nostalgically on his life in the Ford Motor Company! In business you direct a subordinate and manipulate a superior; in politics and in the church you horse-trade, compromise, cajole, persuade. American politics requires one to be as wise as a serpent simply to survive. To be effective, concerned, and honest in getting votes is desperately difficult, occasionally impossible. Joan questions whether the tight victory was worth the cost. But I don't, damn it. Politics is in my blood no matter how I complain.

Second, my taste for business has gone flat. I continue to see the industrial-business complex as an integral strand in our society, salutary to our culture. But a career in business no longer fulfills me. The presidency of our corporation, almost sure to come my way in three years, has lost its mesmerizing attraction. Candidly—pretentiously—I would like to be governor of this state.

I can even see myself as a United States Senator or a Cabinet member! The political careers of Stevenson, Douglas, Percy, and Kerner intrigue me. But I got into politics too late. I should have studied law, entered politics when I was young, and worked up the political ladder. Now, I'm destined to be a drone in the organizational labyrinths of the Party.

Third, working in the upper echelons of our national church, I've been as disillusioned as I was at the congregational level. The inconstancies of human nature in the ecclesiastical hierarchy are discreetly ignored, piously excused, callously denied. At all levels in the church, people are less candid with one another than they are in business or politics. The church has much to learn about simple honesty. Confrontations are run-of-the-mill in the world; they are rare in ecclesiastical circles. Our national board meetings remind me of British politics in the 1930's. Pretense, shallow piety, and blind institutional loyalty insulate lay *and* clerical church leaders against radical self-renewal. Consequently, the bureaucracy bumbles on. I've wondered lately why some churchmen in the 1960's got so excited about finding God in the ambiguities of secular life when the ambiguities in ecclesiastical circles are intensely more evident! From the local presbytery to the offices of the National and World Councils of Churches, the Establishment protects itself against everything—especially genuine renewal.[2]

Fourth, our son has decided suddenly to become a clergyman. Joan and I had no inkling that he was considering any career other than law and politics until he made his abrupt announcement last month. I was incensed and said so loudly. Joan has deep misgivings, too, but insists that Ted be allowed to decide as he chooses. He is cordial with me, respects my judgment in other matters, rejoices in my accomplishments in business and politics, but refuses flatly to re-examine the law, politics, or business as meaningful occupations for him. Both the sudden change in his pursuit of a profession during his last year in college *and* the new goal disturb me. Insisting that he is "called" to be a minister, he resists my pleas to reconsider his vocational decision. I try to be reasonable but fail; a Donnybrook engulfs our household. Joan behaves like a tigress with a threatened cub!

This unpleasant situation is complicated further by his lovely fiancée, Maggi, who supports him in his half-baked decision. Reared with cultural and economic advantages, she hasn't the foggiest notion what she's getting into. Knowing and loving her since she was a towheaded charmer of five, I invited her to lunch several weeks ago expecting to persuade her to talk sense to Ted. But she insisted that she can and will adjust her style of living to fit the demands imposed by any vocation Ted chooses. Gently, she told me that I was trying to live my son's life. I seethed. Graciously, she told me that Joan had reoriented her life to support me first in the corporation and then in politics. I exploded. Maggi had never stood up to me before. I was shocked. But that was only the first round! She told Ted about our luncheon conference. He flew home last weekend and raised hell. The meeting was noisy, nasty, nonproductive. He didn't budge an inch, even when I threatened to cut off his economic support. After he departed, Joan refused to talk with me for the first time in our marriage. I'm confused, frustrated, angry, hurt.

Ted's and Maggi's refusal to re-examine their decision—and Joan's support of them—is disrupting our happy home. This widening breach in our close-knit family is the first and *only* cleavage we've ever experienced. It has shaken my faith. Jeremiah was right: God *is* a deceitful brook. Call Ted in for a conference. Persuade him that his future is not in the church's full-time ministry but in law and politics. Convince him that his decision is unfair to Maggi. Shake some sense into that boy!

Urgently,

Ted

XXXIII

New Canaan
22 November, 1976

Dear Ted,

Most people get bogged down in the Slough of Despond. You've managed to escape that quagmire until now because you gripe constantly and explode periodically. Let's examine the cause of your current malaise.

First, you've engineered a masterful political campaign and won a hard-fought victory. You've demonstrated how to rebuild a political party at the state level. You're bone-tired. The prescription for recovery is simple. Take Joan on a holiday; you both need a change and a rest. Elijah once thought that everyone was faithless—except Elijah. He went petulantly to God, who told him to get a hot meal and go to bed! Elijah recovered; so will you.

Second, you declare that you want to make politics your primary vocation. Yet you insist that at forty-nine it's too late for you. Lincoln, dawdling over life, was almost fifty when he tried for the Senate and lost. Franklin Roosevelt was fifty-one and paralyzed from the waist down when he won the presidency. Stop halting between two opinions. The resolution of your dilemma is simple. Resign from your corporation position; declare your intentions; set out to win support for your candidacy. You certainly have the money to risk it. Eugene McCarthy, Paul Douglas, Frank Graham, and William Fullbright—lacking your economic resources—surrendered their secure positions in the academic community and won elective offices at the national level. Adlai Stevenson, Nelson Rockefeller, and Charles Percy—possessing economic resources— were also successful late-starters in politics. Currently, you are in the nation's eye as a political magician. Newsmen are captivated by your candor and vigor. Your Party is enamored of you. Strike while the iron is hot. You remind me of that medieval martyr who, when asked whether he would have death by flame or on the rack, replied that he would take a little of each!

Third, you complain that your experiences in the upper echelons of your church have disheartened you. I heard *that* complaint years ago when you first got involved in your local church. I've heard it periodically ever since! Nonetheless, you've kept pitching; you've grown into a constructive churchman. What do you expect at any level in the church: medieval saints with halos (illusion), or cagey human beings who live by wit as much as by grace (reality)? Listen to what two Episcopal laymen said about the infamous "Pike Affair" back in 1967. "In recounting these scandals of conscience and heresy, relevance and solemnity in the contemporary Church, in this still unfinished episode, we have found ourselves, as some readers surely will also, alternately outraged and ashamed, amused and bewildered, admiring and cynical, proud and repelled, grateful and chastened. There is much in this account fraught with irony, some that documents stupidity, some which discloses malice, some which glimpses tragedy, some which displays pomposity, some that is filled with humor, some that demonstrates betrayal, and a little which witnesses the power, as well as the need, of forgiveness." [3]

Read again Paul's two Corinthian letters for historical perspective on the church. You've always recognized that the secular city is not the kingdom of God, yet you keep forgetting that the church isn't God's kingdom either. It appears to me that you are trying to separate the wheat from the tares. Your third lament is unbridled petulance.

Now, the fourth lamentation—your son. That handsome, talented, strong-minded lad who rejected *your* plan for *his* life. The strained relationship between you and him is the real cause of your deep-seated weariness, Ted. Your *exhaustion*—induced by a bruising political campaign, a new perspective on vocation, disappointments in church life, *and* middle-age—is natural. You'll recover from it. But your *depression* is caused by the inner conflict generated by your self-willed effort to squeeze your son into a mold of your making. That's the basic cause of your malaise, my friend. Unresolved, it will despoil the creative relationship you have with your son—and disable you.

Actually, in wanting to respect Ted's freedom to decide issues for himself, you're failing to do so. You despise yourself for that failure. Thirty years in teaching young people has convinced me that emotionally healthy youth fight, when necessary, for the freedom to choose mate, vocation, and value structure. Ted, Jr., is fighting you in order to claim a human freedom that is rightfully his. He will not submit to your dictates. He will not respond to your selfish pleas. He will not succumb to your manipulations. And you would disdain him if he did. Tell him frankly that you question his choice of a vocation and why. Tell him also that you will respect *his* freedom to choose as he sees fit—and do precisely that. Stop criticizing God because *you* are mishandling his gift of freedom.

This much I'll say. Ted, Jr., voluntarily made and kept two appointments with me last month. Maggi flew in for the second meeting. The conversations were emotionally honest and reasoned. Your son knows what he is doing. I have said as much to him. One evidence of his emotional maturity and his confidence in his vocational choice is that he did *not* use me to bolster his position during those immature confrontations you engineered. Your son reminds me of another Ted I knew a quarter of a century ago! But this edition is more mature, sensitive, and decisive; less materialistic, arrogant, and opinionated. You did not take Christianity seriously until you were thirty-seven. You changed vocations at fifty. Ted, Jr., at twenty-one, has made a Christian decision that alters his vocational aim and style of life. Give him room to be himself.

Maggi is more realistic and resilient than you realize. You still see her as the little girl who loved and admired you uncritically. She is quite grown up now. With unvarnished candor she acknowledges that she is not personally enamored of

Ted's vocational choice. But her mature love for him motivates her to let him choose the vocation *he* wants, and, like your Joan, to be emotionally supportive to him in his choice. Don't concentrate on *this* aspect of the situation only in terms of the ministry. Many women face and resolve the dilemma inherent in loving a man and being indifferent to or at odds with his vocation (medicine, teaching, military service, corporation life, politics). Some accommodate to the demands of the husband's vocation; others do not. Joan adapted splendidly to both your exacting vocations. She has supported you in every personal venture except your selfish effort to live your son's life. Maggi is that kind of woman, too. Join Joan and her in trusting Ted to choose the vocation that is right for him, for nothing will be right for him unless it is *his* choice.

Humility is a Christian grace that keeps eluding you, old friend. This struggle to let Ted free is the largest test to date in your maturing Christian life. It could be your true "coming of age."

Hopefully,

Jim

Another decade has thundered into history. Jim and Ted have corresponded regularly, met several times a year, and matured as persons in Christ's church. Ted, Jr., a United Presbyterian clergyman, serves a congregation in Denver; he and his wife, Maggi, have two sons, who, according to their grandfather, are destined for politics! Jim, a distinguished professor emeritus, is at work on his magnum opus, Churchill and Hammarskjöld: Political Realists. *Ted, an effective member of two national boards of his church, increasingly a power-*

ful figure in politics, lost a close race in 1982 for governor of his state. Having resigned his corporation vice-presidency prior to that campaign, he then accepted an appointment to the President's Commission on Business and Public Housing. In 1984, Theodore Connors is named as his party's nominee for the United States Senate.

XXXIV

Chicago
10 June, 1984

Dear Jim,

Hemingway once said, "Every man has a girl and her name is nostalgia." That's the girl for me tonight—my only infidelity in thirty-two years of marriage!

It's three decades since I graduated from the University. I remember your asking me at the Phi Beta Kappa banquet if I planned to go on to graduate school and your pained expression when I replied that, tired of thin material advantages, I intended to make money. I set out immediately to achieve that goal. Five corporations, recruiting eagerly, interviewed me. They wanted alert, hard-driving, hungry veterans like me. I chose wisely, worked like a dog, achieved success, gained satisfaction in business and industry, and made money. Investing shrewdly in plastics, electronics, and processed foods, I turned a substantial salary and bonuses into a modest fortune. You know my intimate history over those years.

I'm humbled and exhilarated by the nomination for the Senate. My chances for election are good, but win or lose, I want you to join me. Retirement is not your style. Demonstrate the thesis of your widely acclaimed book, *The Responsibility of Political Power.* Bring your insights and wisdom to bear in fashioning the good society for the sake of the kingdom of God.[4] That's what you challenged me to do years ago; I've never forgotten it. You also taught me to respect the minds of Jefferson, Lincoln, and Wilson; to admire the courage of Jackson, Cleveland, and Robert Taft; to study the style of the Roosevelts and John Kennedy. In spirit, you're already in this campaign; this is your invitation to join in person. Two decades ago intellectuals like Galbraith, Schlesinger, and Sorenson contributed substantially to Stevenson's and Kennedy's salutary impact on American politics. The government needs you. Our party needs you. I need you.

Steve Thomas, one of the associates at Overlook Presbyterian Church fifteen years ago and now a professor of sociology at Notre Dame, phoned yesterday to offer his talent and skills in my campaign. The other associate from those days, Tom Andrews, now the senior minister in an interracial church in Birmingham, phoned his congratulations and good wishes. I regret deeply that Dr. Jameson is not alive to share in this experience. Like you, he allowed me no quarter when I got weary. I think of him often when I'm under pressure.

Years ago, I read Huxley's *Brave New World* and Orwell's *1984!* Now, 1984 is reality. The world is neither a wasteland nor a camp of programmed robots. It's not the horror they envisioned. Huxley and Orwell, like Thomas More, were better writers than prophets. Of course, we don't have One World. International tensions continue to place heavy demands on the political leaders in all nations. As yet, we haven't fashioned a world in which all men are free to become truly human. But the historical possibilities of man *are* unfolding with the promise of a more humane world society. Peaceful coexistence with China and Russia is a present reality and a continuing possibility.

Domestically, our federal government is more responsive to human needs than it was fifty years ago when, under Roosevelt, it provided the motivation and means for accomplishing peacefully a far-reaching socio-economic-political revolution. Today, the federal government is more flexible than it was in the 1960's when it grudgingly provided the political forms to channel the then surging "Civil Rights Revolution" into constructive social changes. The racial revolution has shed its violent character. Black Americans aren't accepted as persons in *all* private social gatherings (who among us is?), but they do experience social and economic justice in *all* public sectors. Their capacity for political leadership is strengthening our political society, too. Seven Negroes are senators, forty-five are serving in the House, one is a Supreme Court Justice, twenty-three are ambassadors, three hold top cabinet posts, thirty or so are city mayors, and thousands are serving on city councils and school boards.

The United Nations—in spite of China's nay votes in the Security Council—functions effectively as a confederation of nations determined to stabilize political situations in regionally troubled areas. Nuclear weapons are under effective international inspection, including those in Red China's arsenal. World opinion is decidedly unsympathetic toward China's chauvinistic nationalism, which is thinly cloaked by an espoused Marxism. Soviet Russia and Japan are quietly allied with Western Europe and the U.S. in helping to develop economically the new nations in Africa and Asia. Of course, Latin America is another "ball game." That seething socio-economic-political caldron—like the Balkans before 1914, central Europe in the 1930s, and Southeast Asia and the Middle

East in the 1950s and 1960s—is the number one challenge to world peace. But there is cause for hope. The "have" nations, especially the United States, are providing technical and economic assistance there without first manipulating the hard-pressed governments to give formal endorsements to "approved" political ideologies. The new openness and political sophistication among this generation of American and European Catholics is particularly helpful in our government's realistic approach to Latin America.

The world is *farther* from Orwell's 1984 than it was in the early 1950s. History, thank God, is not written by IBM machines. Men write history. Concerned, imaginative, responsible men in politics, business, science, education, and religion throughout the world have made countless decisions—wise, short-sighted, compromised—the cumulative effect of which is peaceful coexistence, better understanding and rising cooperation among nations and races, and a larger concern for persons. The United States, learning to use its political and economic power for humane purposes abroad as well as at home, has recovered a measure of the moral leadership it dissipated in 1920-70. I'm excited and sobered by the chance to share in that political leadership. You must participate in it, too. Join us in Chicago.

Now, let me get at the heart of these reminiscences. Jim, there are times when life's unanswerable questions plague me, when the complexities of life bewilder me, when the tragedy of life inundates my hope. My rational mind, grappling with these imponderables, experiences numbing frustration. In fact, my Christian faith sharpens this sense of frustration. One of the relentless questions that nags at me is this: Why was I blessed and burdened with opportunities to be successful, to exercise responsibility in "the corridors of power," and to mature in human relationships in my home and in diverse segments of society? Other people—more deserving and more qualified—have been denied such opportunities. When I think of my contemporaries who were lost in World War II and of the talented youth who were killed in Korea and Vietnam; and when I remember men like Hammarskjold and the Kennedys and King who were cut down before their talents were fully utilized; and when I weep for the hosts of people who, in existential anguish, live daily under "the oppressive weight of the present"—I ask with a mixture of frustration, pain, dread, and awe: Why me?

In my life, and I think in every "favored" life that seeks maturity, personal satisfaction as well as personal failure prods the human spirit to probe the mystery that swirls around man's earthbound existence. Why have I been favored in a world where Golgothas abound? For millions of people, "there are times when life is just awful, boring, stupid, brutal or trivial. The promise of the future does not always, nor can it, drive out the pain of the present. Some people are going to die tomorrow. That is their context, and they want to know why. This is a very personal question, not something that history or sociology or politics can throw much light on. A question like this is wretchedly ultimate, direct, and noncontextual. It just will not go away." [5]

As ever,

Ted

XXXV

New York City
14 June, 1984

Dear Ted,

Anne and I are excited over your nomination for the United States Senate!

I accept eagerly the invitation to serve on your staff. The prospect of having a hand in fashioning political addresses and drafting proposals for public policies is exhilarating. I've envied Galbraith, Keenan, Bundy, Schlesinger, Reischauer, and other academics for years! Today's electorate—backboned by the critical and rebellious youth of the late 1960's—is serious, concerned, knowledgeable, and willing to think for itself *and* for the next generation. You are well equipped for leadership in this hour. You are a political realist without being a cynic. Your Christian perspective enables you to act confidently without certitude. You don't envision a utopian society; you seek a more *humane* society. You will devise practical programs to realize that society; you will compromise responsibly to get those programs implemented. On the other hand, you are not given to political expedience. Principles *and* people matter to you. You communicate that convincingly.

I'm ready to participate in your political campaign, because you are a man who would rather fail immediately with humane programs that will ultimately prevail than one who wants to succeed immediately with shoddy programs that will ultimately fail.[6] You are neither a hard-nosed political realist who disdains "the impossible dream" nor a starry-eyed reformer who only dreams. The former gets society into a rut, while the latter leads society into confusion. Luther once

declared that it would be better to have a wise infidel at the
head of the government than a foolish Christian. That is your
kind of healthy religion.

Now for your question, "Why?" Thomas Carlyle commented
scathingly on philosophical inquiries of this sort: "I don't pre-
tend to understand the universe. It is a great deal bigger than I
am. People ought to be more modest." Nonetheless, people are
not! They want to understand much more than the universe.
And Christians especially, proclaiming a God who acts in history, ask with particular urgency: Why do the "wicked" pros-
per? Why do the "innocent" suffer? Can suffering enrich one's
person? Why me, Lord? and, Why that scandal of a "human"
God?

Asking why God became a man and why it was necessary for
Christ to endure Calvary to accomplish man's liberation, I *decided* years ago that was the only way God could "bridge the
ugly wide ditch" between him and earthbound mortals. To
liberate man he had to use "human history as his instrument." [7] In the man, Jesus, I recognize the true nature and
destiny of man, and in Christ I see enough of the nature and
purpose of God to accept him as Lord. God-in-Christ crossed
the ugly wide ditch to give me a fresh chance to be genuinely
human. Christ is the Truth outside my person who, claimed
in my freedom, liberates me to be what God created me to be—
a man in his image. With others who experience that liberation, I assemble to worship him who sets us free; invigorated,
we go into the world to give and receive, to understand and
to be understood, to forgive and to be forgiven, to love and to
be loved. Christ appeals to others primarily through his fol-
lowers—*new* creatures. But Christians, like other human
creatures, are subject to historical realities.

The first of these realities I call "Fate." Fate is the composite of *time,* which no man ever employs fully or with pure wisdom; *space,* which limits everyone to a particular place at a specific moment; and the *web of human association,* in which each person is inextricably bound.[8] The Christian, like any other human, is subject to time, space, and the web of human association. His historical experience is no more predictable than that of any other person. The essential difference is not *what* happens to him, but *how* he interprets what happens and meets it through Christ's victorious spirit.

Another reality in human existence is individual freedom. Obviously, the degree of any man's freedom is affected by external and internal forces—history and heredity. An artist in Paris is freer to express himself than an artist in Peking. A Negro youth reared by educated, economically solvent parents in Boston has a larger freedom to achieve a superior education than a poverty-ridden Chinese youth reared by unlettered parents in north China. An intellectually gifted, emotionally stable, physically strong person enjoys wider freedom than an intellectually dull, neurotic invalid. A man's freedom is enlarged or limited by his historical situation *and* his heredity. But any normal man's freedom to move toward the light or to cower in the darkness is a viable option in every *human* situation.

Confronted by Christ, man's natural freedom becomes an *event* that constrains him to accept or reject his true humanity. The exercise of that freedom depends on whether he will pay the price to claim the Event. Since God's advent in Christ, man's *highest* freedom is his freedom to be *obedient* to God in serving humanity. When Simon Peter sought to dissuade Jesus from going to Jerusalem, Christ pointed out that he had chosen freely his collision course with Calvary: "No man takes my life from me." He advised Peter that he, Peter, was looking at the situation from man's point of view

—clinging to existence; and not from God's point of view—willing to expend life for others. The essence of human freedom I judge to be this: In Christ, man is enabled to view history from God's point of view *and* to enter actively into God's continuing action to make the world hospitable to humanity.

A third reality then is obedience. Essentially, each human being is free to give his allegiance to whom or what he will. Whatever or whomever one gives himself to places him in an obedient relationship. Freely, the Christian chooses Christ as Lord. Claiming God's promises, he sets out to do Christ's commandments. Claiming God's grace, the Christian is challenged to remember the past correctively and constructively, empowered to meet the present moment heroically and creatively, persuaded that the future belongs to God. The Christian—caught in the web of human association—is motivated to establish truly human relationships and to create humane social-political structures; consequently, he values *his* place in history. Christian freedom *is* voluntary obedience to Christ —choosing to live and die with purpose, rather than just petering out of existence.

At best, however, the Christian's obedience is uneven and his knowledge is imperfect. Faith in Christ does not produce absolute obedience; it does not blot out life's ambiguities; it does not dispel the margins of mystery that surround life. Essentially it is a relationship with Christ that generates insight, understanding, trust, and hope. I can't explain or justify why your life or mine has run steadily while other persons have been cut down by violence, accident, and disease; or been lost to creative leadership in the tangled web of human association. In fact, gospel Faith adds a *new* dimension to man's "Why?" Consider, for example, the serious Christian who lives and dies in an anguished effort to bring hope to the urban ghetto as Martin Luther King did. Why assassination? Consider the serious Christian who lives at the center of the cold war as Joseph Hromadka has. Why defeat?

These concerned leaders *and* their families—and others like them—were and are *driven* to trust that God can and will bring order with justice to society through his continuing activity. Robert Kennedy's plea to his political supporters just before his tragic assassination back in bleak 1968 had this theological overtone: "It is less important what happens to me than what happens to the case I have tried to present." Lincoln's Second Inaugural Address, a political *and* a theological document, owes as much to the Prophets of Israel and the Cross of Christ as it does to the historical situation on 4 March, 1865. B. J. Stiles, Director of Special Projects for the Robert F. Kennedy Memorial Foundation, captured this facet of responsible living: "After the death of Robert Kennedy, I spent some time in South Africa. Still hurt and angered by the absurdity and seeming hopelessness of politics, I was moved deeply by the comment of an Afrikaner writer-politician. He observed, 'When a man gives up faith, he turns to power. When power fails him, he then returns to hope. We have to achieve some balance between our dependence upon power and faith.' " [9]

Whoever seeks to collaborate with God in his world rather than to supplant him will have poignant cause to cry out on occasion: "Why hast thou forsaken me?" The Christian, following Christ in the world, discovers quickly that God's struggle to free the world from incarnate evil is accomplished only through incarnate love and sacrifice. So the Cross becomes both the dynamic and the ground for trust. Nonetheless, there are times and seasons when the Christian finds the historical struggle too much to bear and, yearning for a less demanding existence, denies or flees his Liberator. Occasionally, the Christian plots to betray his Liberator, and, in cold blood, commits that dastardly deed. But the Betrayed seeks out the betrayer. The Father forgives the penitent son. The King offers amnesty to the rebel. The Liberator offers victory to the defeated. And the weary Christian seizes each "given" opportunity to serve Christ anew. Indeed, it is precisely because the kingdom of God is a *gift* that the Christian can accept it as a *task*. It is because God-in-Christ became bone of our bone, sinew of our sinew, flesh of our flesh, that the Christian can claim God's victory in Christ. Dietrich Bonhoeffer appreciated this fully. Burdened with the failure of the bomb plot against Hitler, awaiting execution, he wrote these lines from prison: "This is what I mean by worldliness—taking life in one's stride, with all its duties and problems, its successes and failures, its experiences and helplessness. It is in such a life that we throw ourselves utterly in the arms of God and participate in his sufferings in the world and watch with Christ in Gethsemane." [10]

The Apostle Paul provides the most substantial, and certainly the most concise "answer" to your question—Romans 8:28.

See you in Chicago next week.

Confidently,

Jim

VI

NOTES AND PROFESSOR
JOHNSON'S BIBLIOGRAPHY

*Theological inquiry is not something that
can be added to humanistic and natural-
istic studies; it needs to be constantly informed by them and to inform them.*

—H. RICHARD NIEBUHR

NOTES

INTRODUCTION

[1] Denis de Rougemont, *The Christian Opportunity* (New York: Holt, Rinehart & Winston, 1963), p. 10.

I

[1] News item, *The Lutheran,* March 25, 1968.

[2] *Union Seminary Quarterly Review,* May, 1967, p. 298.

[3] The Congress of Vienna, following the Napoleonic Wars (1815), contributed to European political stability during the nineteenth century.

[4] See "The Hromadka Letter," *Christian Century,* October 2, 1968, p. 1233.

II

[1] This courageous confession of faith clarifies the confessional stance of the United Presbyterian Church on "the Bible and the Word of God," and on the Church and social issues. It supplements the Westminster Confession of 1647; it does *not* supplant it.

[2] See Ben W. Gilbert, *Ten Blocks from the White House: Anatomy of the Washington Riots of 1968* (New York: Praeger, 1968). See also, "Anatomy of a Riot," *Journal of Urban Law,* vol. 45, nos. 3 and 4.

[3] *Markings* (New York: Harper & Row, 1964), p. 15.

III

[1] *No Exit* (Glen Rock, N. J.: Newman Press, 1968), p. 9.

[2] J. Huizinga, *The Waning of the Middle Ages* (New York: Macmillan, 1939), is an intellectual history that may become a classic. It speaks compellingly to "our" moment in history.

[3] *The Children of Light and the Children of Darkness* (New York: Scribner's, 1944), p. xi. Laymen will profit from reading this quarter-century-old study.

[4] Lord Acton, a devout Roman Catholic, was a distinguished nineteenth-century British historian and diplomat whose judgments and decisions were informed by his Faith.

[5] Søren Kierkegaard, a nineteenth-century Danish Lutheran, is the best known Christian existentialist. His violent assertion on the dialectical necessity of correcting every image of God has had an incalculable impact on twentieth-century theology.

[6] See Fisher, *Preface to Parish Renewal.* Chap. 3 provides three approaches for laymen who want to examine biblical and theological descriptions of the church.

[7] John M. Blum, ed., *The National Experience* (New York: Harcourt, Brace & World, 1968), p. 822.

[8] Barzun's speech at a symposium on "The University in America" sponsored by the Center for the Study of Democratic Institutions. Quoted in the *Council for Basic Education Bulletin,* March, 1967.

[9] See Joseph F. Fletcher, *Situation Ethics: The New Morality* (Philadelphia: Westminster Press, 1966), Chap. 4.

[10] See Daniel Callahan, "The Renewal Mess," *Commonweal,* March 3, 1967, p. 622.

[11] (New York: *The Modern Library,* 1951), p. 264.

IV

[1] *Markings,* p. 157.

[2] For a satirical appraisal of manipulation in an English parish, see Auberon Waugh's novel, *Consider the Lilies* (Boston: Little, Brown, 1968). Waugh attacks both the Church of England and Britain's welfare state.

[3] John Galbraith, *The Affluent Society* (Boston: Houghton Mifflin, 1958), p. 322. See also Galbraith's *The New Industrial State* (Houghton Mifflin, 1967).

[4] Harvey Cox, *The Secular City* (New York: Macmillan, Paperbacks, 1965).

[5] R. R. Palmer, *European History* (Princeton: University Press, 1963), p. 139.

[6] Robert Carnot, *Rivers of Blood, Years of Darkness* (New York: Bantam Books, 1967), p. 430.

[7] The study commission was headed by Harvard Law Professor, Archibald Cox. See "Was Violence the Only Way at Columbia?" (editorial report, F.M.H.) *New York Times,* October 10, 1968.

[8] See Fisher, *From Tradition to Mission.* Chaps. 1 through 6 present a clinical study on renewal (12 years) in a historic (240 years) center city church: Trinity, Lancaster, Pennsylvania.

[9] I am indebted to Alfred North Whitehead for this description of worship.

[10] Anders Nygren, *The Significance of the Bible for the Church,* trans. C. C. Rasmussen (Philadelphia: Fortress Press, 1964), p. 36.

[11] See Fisher, *Preaching and Parish Renewal,* pp. 15-32 and 104-7 for a fuller discussion on this issue.

[12] See Arthur A. Rouner, Jr., *The Free Church Today* (New York: Association Press, 1968) for a persuasive plea for dialogue.

[13] This is the bibliography that Professor Johnson compiled for Mr. Connors:

THE CHRISTIAN FAITH

Albright, William F. *From the Stone Age to Christianity.* 2nd ed. Garden City, N.Y.: Doubleday, Anchor Books. 1957.

Anderson, Charles S., ed. *Readings in Luther for Laymen.* Minneapolis: Augsburg, 1967.

Baillie, D. M. *God Was in Christ.* New York: Scribner's, 1948. A classic. Purchase it.

Baillie, John. *Our Knowledge of God.* London: Oxford University Press, 1939.

Bainton, Roland H. *Here I Stand.* Nashville: Abingdon Press, 1950. A classic. Purchase it.

*Barclay, William. *The Mind of Jesus.* New York: Harper, 1961. An excellent introduction for laymen.

*Bonhoeffer, Dietrich. *The Cost of Discipleship,* Translated by by R. H. Fuller. 2nd rev. ed. New York: Macmillan, 1960. Buy it.

Boyd, Malcolm, ed. *The Underground Church.* New York: Sheed & Ward, 1968.

Buber, Martin. *I and Thou.* Translated by R. Gregor Smith. 2nd ed. New York: Scribner's, 1958. A classic. Purchase it.

*Bultmann, Rudolf. *Kerygma and Myth.* New York: Harper, Torchbooks. 1961. Study especially "New Testament and Mythology."

Cox, Harvey. *On Not Leaving It to the Snake.* New York: Macmillan, 1967.

Davies, D. R. *Secular Illusion or Christian Realism?* 2nd ed. rev. New York: Macmillan, 1953. A concise differentiation for the thoughtful layman.

*Ebeling, Gerhard. *The Nature of Faith.* Translated by R. G. Smith. Philadelphia: Fortress Press, 1962. Study this work diligently. It was written for *you.* Purchase it.

*————. *Word and Faith.* Philadelphia: Fortress Press, 1963. A concise statement. Purchase it.

Hordern, William. *A Layman's Guide to Protestant Theology.* Rev. ed. New York: Macmillan, 1968. An excellent introduction for laymen. Purchase it.

Hunter, Archibald M. *The Message of the New Testament.* Philadelphia: Westminster Press, 1944. The book is a quarter-century old, but it offers nonprofessionals a solid introduction to New Testament literature.

Jenkins, Daniel. *The Strangeness of the Church.* Garden City, N. Y.: Doubleday, 1955.

Knox, John. *Myth and Truth.* Charlottesville: University Press of Virginia, 1964.

Macquarrie, John. *The Scope of Demythologizing.* London: SCM Press, 1960.

Mowinckel, Sigmund. *The Old Testament as Word of God.* Translated by Reidar Bjornard. Nashville: Abingdon Press, 1959.

*Niebuhr, H. Richard. *Christ and Culture.* New York: Harper, Torchbooks. 1956. Study carefully chapters 1, 5, and 6.

————. *The Responsible Self.* New York: Harper, 1963.

Niebuhr, Reinhold. *Faith and History.* New York: Scribner's, 1949.

*Oman, John. *Grace and Personality.* New York: Association

Press, Giant Reflection Book, 1961. A theological classic. Purchase it.

Read, David H. C. *The Christian Faith*. Apex Books; Nashville: Abingdon Press, 1969. A solid, brief statement on the elements of the Christian religion.

*Robinson, H. Wheeler. *Two Hebrew Prophets*. Naperville, Ill.: Allenson, 1948.

*Temple, William. *Christianity and Social Order*. London: SCM Press, 1950. Read it twice!

Tillich, Paul. *Morality and Beyond*. New York: Harper, 1963.
————. *The Courage to Be*. New Haven: Yale University Press, 1952. Purchase it.

*————. *Love, Power, and Justice*. New York: Oxford University Press, 1954.

*————. *The New Being*. New York: Scribner's 1955. Purchase it.

*Tournier, Paul. *The Meaning of Persons*. New York: Harper, 1957. Study Parts I and II—"The Personage" and "The Person."

*Wingren, Gustaf. *Theology in Conflict*. Translated by Eric H. Wahlstrom. Philadelphia: Fortress Press, 1958.

Wright, G. Ernest. *The Biblical Doctrine of Man in Society*. London: SCM Press, 1954.

CHRISTIANITY AND CULTURE

*Allport, Gordon. *Becoming: Basic Considerations for a Psychology of Personality*. New Haven: Yale University Press, 1955. This is an invaluable book. Purchase it.

*Barzun, Jacques. *The House of Intellect*. New York: Harper, Torchbooks, 1959.

Bell, Daniel. *The End of Ideology*. New York: The Free Press, 1959.

*Brinton, Crane. *The Anatomy of Revolution*. New York: Vintage, 1957. Read it for perspective on contemporary revolutions.

*Brogan, Denis. *The American Character*. New York: Knopf, 1944. Read Part I especially, the feminization of American culture.

Bruckberger, Raymond L. *The Image of America*. New York: Viking Press, 1959. This is a French Dominican priest's attempt to understand "America as a reality." He appreciates the American industrialists' contribution to society.

Calhoun, Robert C. *God and the Day's Work*. New York: Association Press, Reflection Book, 1957.

Callahan, Daniel, ed., *The Secular City Debate*. New York: Macmillan, Paperback, 1966.

*Commager, Henry Steele. *The American Mind*. New Haven: Yale University Press, a Yale Paperbound, 1950. Purchase this indispensable historical study of American thought and character since the 1880's.

*Cox, Harvey, ed., *The Situation Ethics Debate*. Philadelphia: Westminster Press, 1968. See especially, Edward Leroy Long, Jr., "The History and Literature of 'The New Morality'," pp. 101-16; and Henlee H. Barnette, "The New Ethics: 'Love Alone'," pp. 121-40.

Dawson, Christopher H. *The Historical Reality of Christian Culture*. New York: Harper, 1960.

Fletcher, Joseph. *Situation Ethics*. Philadelphia: Westminster Press, 1966. You will find it fascinating, enlightening, irritating!

*Galbraith, John Kenneth. *The Affluent Society*. Boston: Houghton Mifflin, 1958.

*———. *The New Industrial State*. Boston: Houghton Mifflin, 1967.

*Gardner, John W. *Excellence: Can We Be Equal and Excellent Too?* New York: Harper, 1961.

Greeley, Andrew. *The Crucible of Change*. New York: Sheed & Ward, 1968. A Roman Catholic priest-sociologist's views on tradition and change

Hartt, Julian N. *A Christian Critique of American Culture*. New York: Harper, 1967.

*Hofstadter, Rochard. *Anti-Intellectualism in American Life*. New York: Knopf, 1963. Purchase this one, and read it carefully.

*Howe, Reuel L. *The Miracle of Dialogue*. New York: Seabury Press, 1963. An excellent introduction.

Hughes, Everett C. *Men and Their Work*. Chicago: University of Chicago Press, 1959.

Kohn, Hans. *Nationalism, Its Meaning and History*. Princeton: Van Nostrand, 1955. Indispensable for responsible citizenship.

Lasch, Christopher. *The New Radicalism in America*, 1889-1962. New York: Knopf, 1965. A study of the intellectual as a social type (e.g. Jane Addams, Walter Lippmann, Reinhold Niebuhr, Norman Mailer, Sydney Hook).

Latourette, Kenneth Scott. *Christianity Through the Ages*. New York: Harper, 1965.

Long, Edward Leroy. *Conscience and Compromise: An Outline of Protestant Casuistry*. Philadelphia: Westminster Press, 1954.

Marcuse, Herbert. *One-Dimensional Man*. Boston: Beacon Press, 1964.

Miller, William Lee. *The Protestant and Politics*. Philadelphia: Westminster Press, 1958. An excellent introduction.

*Murray, Michael H. *The Thought of Teilhard de Chardin*. New York: Seabury Press, 1966.

Niebuhr, Reinhold. *Pious and Secular America*. New York: Scribner's, 1958.

Northrop, F. S. C. *The Meeting of East and West*. New York: Macmillan, Paperbacks, 1960. Purchase it.

Overstreet, Harry and Bonaro. *The Strange Tactics of Extremism*. New York: W. W. Norton, 1964.

*Ramsey, Michael. *Canterbury Essays and Addresses*. New York: Seabury Press, 1964.

Russell, Bertrand. *Why I Am Not a Christian*. New York: Simon and Schuster, 1957.

Tawney, R. H. *Religion and the Rise of Capitalism*. New York: Harcourt, Brace & World, 1947. Purchase it.

*Ulam, Adam B. *Expansion and Coexistence: The History of Soviet Foreign Policy, 1917-67*. New York: Praeger, 1968.

Van Buren, Paul. *The Secular Meaning of the Gospel*. New York: Macmillan, 1963.

Vidler, Alec R., ed., *Soundings*. New York: Cambridge University Press, 1962.

*Ward, Barbara. *Five Ideas that Change the World*. New York: W. W. Norton, 1959. A concise presentation on nationalism, industrialism, colonialism, communism, and internationalism. Purchase it.

West, Rebecca. *The New Meaning of Treason*. New York: Viking Press, 1964.

(Of course, you will sample twentieth-century writers and playwrights: James Baldwin, Saul Bellow, Robert Bolt, Albert Camus, James Cozzens, T. S. Eliot, William Faulkner, Herbert

Gold, Paul Goodwin, Graham Greene, Ernest Hemingway, Rolf Hochhuth, Norman Mailer, Mary McCarthy, Arthur Miller, John O'Hara, John Osborne, Boris Pasternak, J. D. Salinger, Jean-Paul Sartre, John Updike, Tennessee Williams, Herman Wouk, Robert Penn Warren, and others.)

STUDIES ON CHRISTIAN FUTURITY

Baum, Gregory, ed., *The Future of Belief Debate*. New York: Herder and Herder, 1967.

Bennett, John, Cox, Harvey, *et al.* Symposium, "Christian Realism," *Christianity And Crisis,* August 5, 1968.

*Bultmann, Rudolf. *History and Eschatology*. New York: Harper, Torchbooks, 1957. Tackle it.

Dewart, Leslie. *The Future of Belief*. New York: Herder and Herder, 1966.

*Marty, Martin. *The Search for a Usable Future*. New York: Harper, 1969. A solid introduction to "futurism."

*Moltmann, Jürgen. *Theology of Hope*. Translated by James W. Leitch. New York: Harper, 1967. Tackle it.

Pannenberg, Wolfhart. *Jesus: God and Man*. Translated by Lewis L. Wilkins and Duane Priebe. Philadelphia: Westminster Press, 1958. Tackle it.

Rahner, Karl. *The Christian of the Future*. New York: Herder and Herder, 1967. A Roman Catholic theologian (German) who will fascinate you.

*Schillebeeckx, E., O. P., *God: The Future of Man*. New York: Sheed & Ward, 1968. Quite readable. Another Roman Catholic theologian (Dutch) who will stimulate your thinking.

*Teilhard de Chardin, Pierre. *The Phenomenon of Man*. New York: Harper, 1959. Purchase it.

———. *The Future of Man*. New York: Harper, 1964.

NEWSPAPERS

Subscribe to *The New York Times, The Christian Science Monitor,* and *The Manchester Guardian.* Ask friends and colleagues to provide articles (on subjects which interest you) from a wide range of magazines. Maintain a select file.

---

[14] (New York: Harcourt, Brace & World, 1968.)

[15] *Ibid.,* p. 30.

[16] *Ibid.,* p. 31.

[17] Blum, *The National Experience,* p. 842.

[18] Richard Hofstadter, *The American Political Tradition and the Men Who Made It* (New York: Knopf, 1967), Introduction, p. v. See also Henri Bergson, *The Two Sources of Morality and Religion* (New York: Harper, 1935). Chaps. I and II provide an enlightening discussion on the role of conservatism in culture. For a recent Roman Catholic view from Ireland, see J. P. Mackey, *Tradition and Change in the Church* (Dayton, Ohio: Pflaum Press, 1968). The inevitability, necessity, disadvantages, and advantages of tradition are discussed, pp. 150-92.

[19] Blum, *The National Experience,* p. 845.

[20] Gerhard Ebeling, *God and Word,* trans. James W. Leitch (Philadelphia: Fortress Press, 1964), p. 45.

[21] Marshall McLuhan, *Understanding Media: The Extensions of Man* (New York: The New American Library, n.d.), p. 85.

[22] Fisher, *Preface To Parish Renewal,* Chap. 2, "By Whose Authority?" provides a critical approach to the Scriptures in non-technical language.

[23] Updike, *The Same Door* (New York: Fawcett, 1959), p. 80.

[24] The Machen controversy at Princeton provided the historical context in which Carl McIntire's views on the scriptures were framed.

[25] William Stringfellow and Anthony Towne, *The Bishop Pike Affair* (New York: Harper, 1967) is a documented, lively account of ecclesiastical politics. See also the Rev. Lester Kinsolving's column, *Religion Today,* Pittsburgh Post Gazette, Saturday, Oct. 12, 1968, "Sweep It Under the Rug," a critical report on the trial of Bishop Joseph Minnis in Denver, Colorado, 1968. See also Stephen F. Bayne, Jr., chairman, *Theological Freedom and Social Responsibility* (New York: Seabury Press, 1967). The report of the advisory committee of the Episcopal Church appointed by the Presiding Bishop, the Rt. Rev. John E. Hines, on January 12, 1967, "to advise him in relation to the theological situation with which the Episcopal Church is faced" (Introduction: The Charge to the Advisory Committee, p. 3.).

[26] Quoted, John Wilkins, "The Church in a Secular Age," in *The Restless Church,* William Kilbourn, ed. (Philadelphia: Lippincott, 1966), p. 49.

[27] *Ibid.* See also M. M. Thomas, "The Church in a Revolutionary World," *The Ecumenical Review* (Quarterly, the World Council of Churches), Oct. 1968, pp. 410-19.

[28] Sydney Mead, *The Lively Experiment* (New York: Harper, 1967).

[29] Quoted, Robert M. Hutchins, "Permanence and Change," *The Center* magazine, Sept., 1968, p. 5.

[30] Cox, *The Secular City,* p. 256.

[31] Reinhold Niebuhr, *The Nature and Destiny of Man* vol. I (New York: Scribner's, 1942), p. 5.

[32] Blaise Pascal, *Pensées,* Louis Lafuma, ed., John Warrington, tr. (New York: E. P. Dutton, 1960), p. 65.

V

[1] Herbert Butterfield, *Man on His Past* (Boston: Beacon Press, 1966), pp. 126-28. For a critique of the view that politics provides media for effective Christian witness, see Will D. Campbell and James Y. Holloway, "Up to Our Steeple in Politics," *Christianity and Crisis,* March 3, 1969, pp. 36-40.

[2] Stephen Rose, *The Grass Roots Church* (Nashville: Abingdon Press, Apex ed., 1966) presents a sharp indictment against the rigidity of institutional denominationalism.

[3] Stringfellow and Towne, *The Bishop Pike Affair,* p. 6.

[4] Daniel D. Williams, *God's Grace and Man's Hope* (New York: Harper, 1950) develops this thesis persuasively for the thoughtful layman.

[5] Daniel Callahan, ed; *The Secular City Debate* (New York: Macmillan, 1966), p. 99.

[6] I am indebted to Woodrow Wilson for this incisive description of practical idealism.

[7] J. S. Whale, *Christian Doctrine* (New York: Macmillan, 1941), p. 59.

[8] I am indebted to Werner Elert for this description of Fate.

[9] B. J. Stiles, "Variety of Ministries," *Christianity and Crisis,* March 3, 1969, p. 43.

[10] Dietrich Bonhoeffer, *Letters and Papers from Prison* (New York: Macmillan, 1962), p. 169.